# MINI FASHION

## SEW CLOTHES FOR BABIES & TODDLERS

Jules Naht

IN SIZES
50–104
(BABY TO 4/5 YEARS)
&
2 DOUBLE-SIDED
PATTERN SHEETS

# CONTENTS

## AUTUMN | WINTER

## INTRODUCTION

*"We must teach our children to smell the earth, to taste the rain, to touch the wind, to see things growing, to hear the sunrise and to care."*

Anonymous

Today, if you philosophise about fashion, you will soon encounter terms, such as sustainability, slow fashion, fair fashion and organic certification. The trend is huge, and the market is booming so it is all the more important that all of us make our small or large contributions. As a mother, I want to set an example and to make my children aware of these ideas; in the end they constantly surround us in our daily lives. My passion is handmade and that is where I want to contribute or at least try to.

Nowadays, there are gorgeous organic fabrics, and they are even affordable, which I consider a great step forward. You can find really nice material from certified organic manufactures at www.echtanziehend.de.

The fabric is one thing, but you also have to be consistent in terms of sustainable design.

My designs are casual and intended to grow with your child. Maybe your pieces could be worn by several children. They are intended to give you and your little one enjoyment for as long as possible and can be combined easily. Muted colours, minimalistic style and little fuss – that is how I like it.

I am looking forward to seeing how you like it too...

**TIP:**
*Use the hashtag #minifashion on Instagram to show us your finished items.*

# PROJECT GALLERY

## SPRING | SUMMER

**BLOOMERS**
**P.41**

**MUSLIN SHIRTS**
**P.45**

**MUSLIN SWEATER**
**P.49**

**ROMPER**
**P.53**

**SHIRT WITH BUTTON PLACKET**
**P.59**

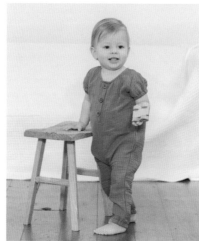

**OVERALL**
**P.65**

**DUNGAREES**
**P.71**

**PIXIE HAT**
**P.79**

**MUSLIN SLEEPING BAG**
**P.83**

**BATHING PONCHO**
**P.89**

RIB KNIT BODYSUIT
P.95

TROUSERS WITH BUTTON PLACKET
P.99

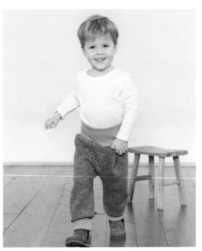

BAGGY TROUSERS
P.103

BOILED WOOL WRAP-AROUND JACKET
P.107

RIB KNIT LEGGINGS
P.111

BOILED WOOL MINI JACKET
P.115

BOILED WOOL PLAYSUIT
P.125

BOILED WOOL MINI HAT
P.133

BEANIE
P.137

# WHEN YOUR FINGERS ITCH AND CREATIVITY OVERCOMES REASON

That is exactly how crafters feel, when a creative thought fills their mind. Nothing else matters except focusing on the idea, all other thoughts are blocked out and your hands take control. This state of mind arises from my passion for creating things with my own two hands, for making something new and for expressing my own creativity.

I love this feeling and remember experiencing it right back in my early childhood. I would spend hours crafting, creating, painting and trying out new ideas with my mother, and so at some point, I wound up working with textiles and sewing.

After starting off hand stitching, I was soon allowed to use my mother's sacred sewing machine. It awoke a great passion that has not yet left me.

Today, around thirty years later, this machine is still in use when its digital companions break down (it is rarely the case, but it has happened).

After the birth of our second daughter and my subsequent motherhood comprising housework, cooking, cleaning and changing nappies, I really needed time for me, time for my passion, time to let my creativity flow and time for relaxation.

"Sewing was my relief" – I can't think of a more fitting way to put it. There was really nothing nicer than being approached on the street or by a friend about a homemade item – they were moments of pure happiness.

With my third child, everything sped up a little – my husband and I established the children's fashion label JULESNaht.

Simple design, muted colours, Scandinavian peacefulness and minimalism, which is what we love. We use fabrics, such as muslin, linen, corduroy and boiled wool.

In this book, we are taking you on a journey full of beautiful, easy-to-make and very practical projects. You will find simple designs, which depending upon the fabric can be used in many situations and that will make your little one look as sweet as sugar from spring to winter in one-of-a-kind garments.

**HI!**

How lovely that you are here! I hope you get a lot of enjoyment out of this book, which is so dear to me.

# BASICS, TIPS AND TRICKS

With dressmaking, as so often in life, the saying "practice makes perfect" is true. If you are an experienced hobby seamstress, then you will know what I mean. If you are an absolute beginner, you are about to find out. Whatever your level of proficiency, this book must have appealed to you, and so you are in exactly the right place.

Even after many years of dressmaking, there are still times when something feels impossible to work out and despair is near, however, the joy returns the exact moment that it all falls into place. I want you to experience such moments and so in many places in this book, I offer my personal experience in order to help you.

I personally like uncomplicated things and love designs that give me beautiful results quickly and without fuss. I have fed this into the designs and how to sew them. If you like this simplicity, then just follow the patterns and if you would like the clothing to be more elaborate, then the designs in this book also allow you plenty of room to experiment.

In due course, you should have created many beautiful pieces of clothing and be able to take this book from the shelf with joy, whenever you feel like a sewing project.

This is my
IS MY
HAPPY
PLACE

74/80

12

BOILED WOOL

WAFFLE COTTON

COTTON WEAVE

RIB KNIT

SEERSUCKER

LINEN

MUSLIN

# THE FABRIC FROM WHICH DREAMS ARE MADE

You have to touch fabric; you have to feel it and you have to place your hands on it to understand it. Cosy, fluffy, soft, woolly, cooling and comfortable – fabric is all of the above and much more. Fabric in its diversity is indescribably beautiful and almost marvellous in its appeal. My heart beats for woven fabrics, which feature heavily in this book. How wonderful that right now this fabric is once again making many hearts beat faster and its admirers are increasingly growing in number.

The reason for this development is the current trendsetter in the woven fabric department: muslin. On top of muslin, this book also has patterns that use linen, waffle cotton, corduroy, seersucker and elastic fabric such as jersey and rib knit.

For the colder seasons, we use my absolute favourite fabric: boiled wool. I simply love it. Why? I will let you know in due course.

Upon selecting your material, every sewing project becomes your own. Therefore, take your time in choosing your fabric. Above all allow your inner eye to inspire you, and the results will be all the more beautiful.

But before that, let's take a small detour into the broad and wonderful world of fabric.

**TIP:**
You can find an enchanting selection of high quality and beautiful organic fabrics at the fabric seller echt-anziehend (www.echtanziehend.de).

## LINEN AND LINEN MIX

Linen has been well-known and well-loved for hundreds of years. This fabric is also currently celebrating its comeback in children's fashion. Not only does it give clothes an elegant summer look, but it exhibits great properties, such as a cooling effect in the summer. Linen is produced from the fibres of the flax plant and can be combined with a large variety of other materials or used as pure linen. As a rule of thumb, the higher the linen percentage in the fabric, the sturdier and more susceptible to creasing it is. Linen itself is not elastic, but it is now available with added elastane, which is wonderful for use in children's fashion.

### FACTS

» *Linen shrinks a lot! Therefore, it must be washed before cutting. Remember the shrinkage when calculating how much fabric to buy.*

» *You may iron linen, but you don't have to. There is a reason for the German saying, "linen creases elegantly".*

» *When cutting the fabric, it is necessary to follow the run of the thread.*

» *Linen lies very flat, and you must work carefully when cutting it.*

» *When cutting linen, ensure you observe the seam allowance exactly. Linen frays a lot and must always be finished.*

» *You can also use an overlocker to sew linen but pay attention that you will also need to resew all seams with a sewing machine so that they have the necessary stability. In this way, the stitches will have a very neat appearance, and everything will be secure.*

» *Use a size 70 universal needle and a stitch length of 2-3 mm.*

# MUSLIN

At the moment, this enchanting cotton fabric is on trend for all kinds of clothing for children and adults alike. Its fan base is increasing, and more and more patterns are coming on to the market to sew wonderful muslin creations.

Just two years ago, I would get funny looks because my son had the typical "burp cloth" material sewn into his jacket, but now we get envious glances when my daughter wears her chic muslin dress.

Muslin is a loosely woven double weave made from cotton. It has a soft and fluffy feel and is incredibly practical.

Thanks to the way muslin is made, small pockets of air are formed and give the fabric its typical crinkle look. Muslin should not be ironed. Tumble drying highlights its structure. How practical for us busy mothers.

## FACTS

» *Muslin shrinks a lot! Therefore, it must be washed before cutting. Remember the shrinkage when calculating how much fabric to buy.*

» *A 3 to 3.5 mm stitch length is perfect for muslin, sometimes it is also necessary to reduce the presser foot pressure on your sewing machine.*

» *Be careful that the lower feed dog does not damage the weave on removal. At this point, I like to use the automatic lowering, otherwise the handwheel helps.*

» *Use a size 70 universal or jersey needle.*

» *Finish the edges with a zigzag stitch or the overlocker.*

» *You can also use an overlocker to sew muslin but ensure that you are actually sewing through both layers of fabric, and nothing slips.*

» *Finally, I always use the sewing machine to strengthen seams that have to withstand some strain, such as crotch seams, by adding an additional seam.*

## OTHER COTTON MATERIALS

**Seersucker** is a cotton fabric that does not require ironing thanks to its ruffled, crepe-like surface. It is perfect for the warmer seasons.

Often, its special weave becomes a feature through the colour selection of the threads.

It is available in particularly pretty striped and check patterns but also in plain colours. You can use **seersucker** to create cute romper suits, shorts, light blouses and dresses.

**Waffle cotton** is a soft but relatively hard-wearing fabric that can have a variety of honeycomb appearances. The unique waffle structure of this cotton fabric, which is also non-iron, creates an on-trend look that can lend simple designs that certain something. It works for nearly all projects, and it can be used to sew jackets, trousers or dresses in next to no time.

**Corduroy** goes through a manufacturing process that gives it its typical velvet-like ribs. Corduroy can have both wide and thin ribs. It is currently enjoying great popularity. Stretch corduroy with a small percentage of elastane is a great alternative and perfectly suited for cute mini fashion.

### FACTS

» *You should always prewash cotton fabrics.*

» *Raw edges should always be finished.*

» *You can also use an overlocker to sew cotton fabric but pay attention that you additionally resew all seams using a sewing machine so that they have the necessary stability. In this way, the stitches will have a very neat appearance, and everything will be secure.*

» *Use a size 70 universal needle and a stitch length of 2-3 mm.*

## KNITTED FABRICS

**Jersey, French terry** and **sweatshirt** fabric are extremely popular types of fabric. In their unlimited variety of appearance and feel, they are absolute all-rounders for children's fashion. Comfortable, snuggly, thick, thin, colourful or simple – whatever your heart desires.

Their high elasticity stems from the manufacturing process. A rotary cutting tool is well suited to cut them and they should be sewn with a stitch length of 2-3 mm.

**Rib knit or jersey rib:** this kind of fabric has many names as does the composition of fibres used to produce it. We are however in agreement about one thing – it is totally on trend. When purchasing, try to get a fabric with a high cotton percentage.

### FACTS

» *You do not need to finish jersey.*

» *When cutting, observe the direction of the run of the thread.*

» *It can be sewn with zigzag stitch or using the overlocker.*

» *Use jersey needles. As a rule of thumb: the thinner the jersey, the thinner the needle should be.*

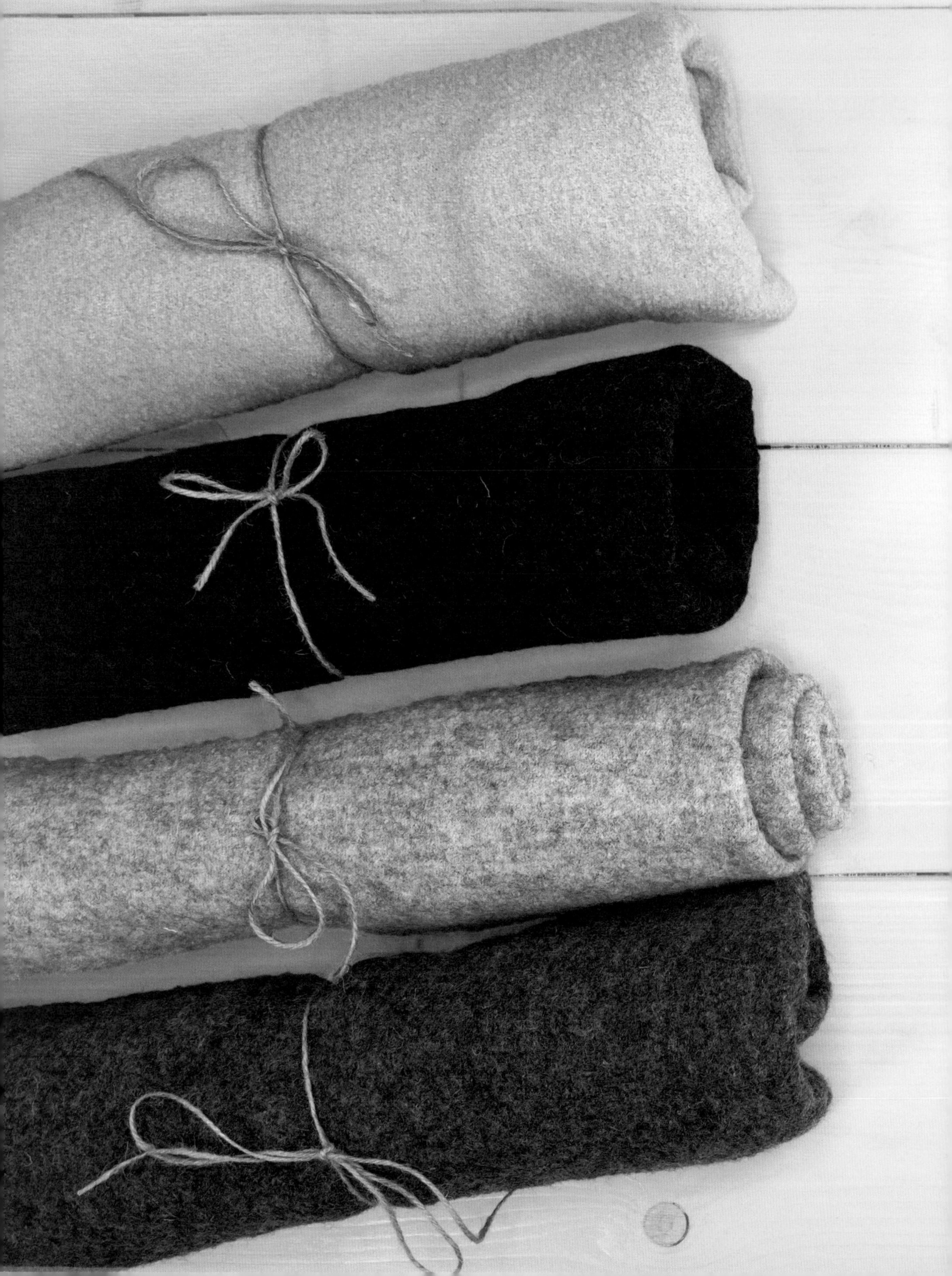

# BOILED WOOL

As I have already told you: I love boiled wool.

It is not only the best material for dressing your little one from autumn to spring, but it is also a joy to work with.

The new wool has the perfect attributes to allow small children to enjoy wild games outdoors in the colder months and to stay nice and warm while walking in the fresh air.

Boiled wool is an untreated material that is extremely well suited for making clothes for babies and children. It is flexible, not too thick, moves with them and still keeps the little ones toasty warm.

Boiled wool (knitted before boiling) and loden (woven before boiling) are very similar and are both created from sheep's wool. During the manufacturing process, countless small air chambers are formed that give the material its typical "felted" appearance.

The quality of boiled wool is varied and can be determined according to its weight. For suits and jackets, I only use 415 gsm boiled wool. This thick fabric offers protection against wind and weather.

## FACTS

» *Boiled wool regulates your temperature, stores body heat, absorbs a lot of damp without getting wet and is very durable, dirt-repellent and self-cleaning.*

» *When purchasing, pay attention to the percentage of wool. I personally only use boiled wool made of 100% wool.*

» *You do not need to finish boiled wool; it can even be worked with raw edges.*

» *Use a jersey needle for sewing.*

» *It is personal preference whether you use the overlocker or a conventional sewing machine. Just ensure that when using the overlocker that the seams are very thick.*

» *You can even wash boiled wool in the washing machine. The COLD cycle does not damage the material. It is important to use a good laundry detergent and NOT to spin it. After washing, it is best to lay it flat on a towel to dry.*

# IMPORTANT TOOLS

*There is an incredible number of tools on the market and new products are appearing daily. In this regard, I also work according to the principal "less is more" and limit myself to the tools that are essential for me.*

### VARIO PLIERS

These pliers are used to quickly and easily attach press studs to your clothing.

### HAND AND SEAM GAUGE

Different to a normal ruler, the measurement marks on the hand and seam gauge start right at the lower edge. Therefore, it can be positioned directly at the edge of the fabric. It allows wonderful straight and precise measurements and the marking of optimal seam allowances and hems.

### PATCHWORK RULER

When working with the rotary cutting tool (patchwork) rulers are a useful tool. They are more solid and heavier than normal rulers and have a nonslip surface which allows them to remain in place on the fabric while cutting. They are well suited for both long and short cuts.

### SELF-ERASING MARKERS AND CHALK

You can use self-erasing markers or chalk to trace the markings from the pattern on to the fabric. The markings made with self-erasing markers disappear after a while and you can carefully brush off the chalk.

### PAPER SCISSORS

An all-rounder for cutting anything that is not fabric, for example for cutting out the pattern.

## DRESSMAKING SCISSORS

When cutting material, you should always use fabric or dressmaking scissors. They are different to normal scissors and their flat underside makes it possible to position them flat on the table allowing them to cut the fabric smoothly and without puckering. Good dressmaking scissors glide through the material and cutting becomes child's play.

It is very important that you ONLY cut fabric with them. If you use them for anything else, you will quickly regret it.

## SEAM RIPPER

A small, loyal helper, when a seam isn't where it is supposed to be. This clever tool saves a lot of frustration when unpicking such misplaced seams. Incidentally, it is also a perfect solution for opening buttonholes (you can find instructions for buttonholes on page 26).

## EMBROIDERY SCISSORS

They are perfect for cutting threads and making pattern notches.

## SMALL/LARGE ROTARY CUTTER

As a useful option, I recommend a rotary cutter. With a little bit of practice, you can use it to carefully and above all quickly cut out your pieces. Always use the rotary cutter in combination with a cutting mat.

Rotary cutters or scissors – that is a matter of personal preference. Try out both to see which suits you best.

## CUTTING MAT

A cutting mat protects your table top when using a rotary cutter. It is made of a special material that "heals" itself after you have cut over it. Cutting mats should be stored flat so that they do not bend or become misshapen. They are available in various sizes. To begin with, a 90 x 60 cm mat is perfect.

# HELPFUL MATERIALS

### PATTERN PAPER

You need pattern paper to transfer the pattern from the pattern sheets on to the fabric so that you can sew the design in the correct size. It is best to use a permanent marker to transfer the pattern.

### SAFETY PIN

In your projects, you will use this all-rounder in order to thread elastic through a waistband or hem.

### SEWING MACHINE NEEDLES

To save myself from the rabbit hole of sewing machine needles, I have limited myself to universal needles and size 70 jersey needles for this book. If you use an overlocker, then size 80 overlocking needles are the right choice.

### SEWING COTTON

Regarding sewing cotton, your primary concern should be quality. Cheap cotton snaps and frays easily, which causes frustration and hampers good results. For the projects in this book, you will be well equipped with polyester cotton. This cotton can sew anything, is robust and is somewhat elastic making it perfectly suited for cotton, wool and knitted fabrics.

### PINS AND FABRIC CLIPS

In order to hold fabric together, you can use pins or fabric clips. You should have both at your work station, for sometimes you can't do without the good old pin.

### WEIGHTS

If you find pinning your pattern to your fabric too laborious, then weights are a good alternative for you. Instead of pinning, you simply place the small weights over the pattern and fabric to prevent sliding when you are tracing the pattern or directly cutting out the piece.

## ELASTIC

For some of the projects in this book, you will need elastic with a width of 1 or 2 cm in order to create waistbands or hems.

## PRESS STUDS

The fastening all-rounder. They allow clothes to be quickly undone and done up again. For woven fabric you can use "jersey press studs". Press studs are pushed through the material using pliers or a special tool. For thin fabric, e.g., muslin, you will need to add interfacing so that the studs do not easily rip out.

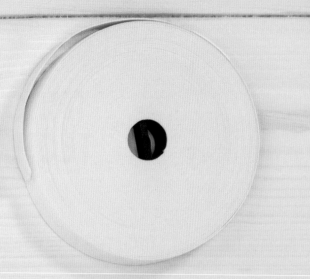

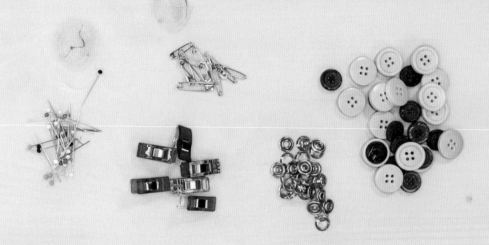

## IRON-ON INTERFACING

Iron-on interfacing is used to lend fabric a certain stability. It can be used for the majority of fabrics and is available in various thicknesses. For the projects in this book, we will only use H200 and H250 interfacing.

Use H200 interfacing to strengthen thin fabrics, e.g., muslin, linen or seersucker, around the buttons. In this book, the H250 interfacing is used for the button placket on the boiled wool jacket and the boiled wool playsuit. Always iron the interfacing on to the lining because the boiled wool is not heat resistant. The fusible side of the interfacing is identifiable because it has a slight shine. To protect the material when you iron it on, you should place a towel or a piece of grease proof paper between the clothing and the iron.

## WOODEN BUTTONS

As well as being useful for fastening, you can also use wooden buttons for decoration. However, be careful because wooden buttons may stain fabric. Therefore, we recommend you do a wash test. To do so, simply sew one of the buttons on to some leftover material and pop it into the washing machine.

Important: Since we are making clothes for little ones, ensure that the wooden buttons and press studs are safely and securely attached.

# IMPORTANT TECHNIQUES

## FINDING THE RIGHT STITCH FOR EVERY FABRIC

There are so many different options for sewing and seaming. As a rule of thumb, use universal needles for woven fabric and jersey needles for elastic fabric and boiled wool.

Sew woven wear using a normal straight stitch **(image 1)** with a stitch length of 2-3 mm. You will need to secure each seam by sewing three to four stitches forwards, backwards and then forwards again at the start and end. Today, many machines have an automatic function that secures the ends. It's a feature you can quickly get used to.

When sewing woven fabric, finishing is essential. A sewing machine allows you to finish using a normal zig-zag stitch **(image 2)**. This step can be done before sewing (all pieces of the pattern are individually finished) or it can be done right at the end. If you want seams that you can iron flat, then you should finish the pieces individually.

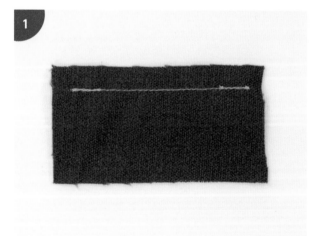

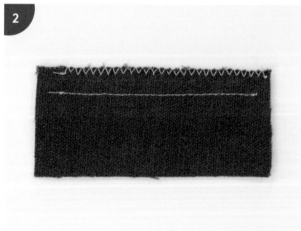

It is easiest to use an overlocker **(image 3)**. However, for woven fabric you should also stabilise all seams with an additional straight stitch.

In this book, we also use the stretch stitch for raw edges on boiled wool **(image 4)**.

As decoration, I like to use the triple straight stitch for small sew-on snappap patches **(image 5)**.

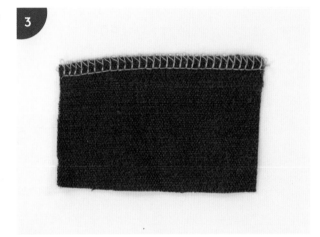

# SEWING BUTTONHOLES

Whatever method you use, ironing on interfacing around the buttonholes is highly recommended. It gives you a beautiful buttonhole with a high-end appearance, rip-resistance and stability. For sewing buttonholes with and without a buttonhole foot, you will need a hand gauge, pins and a self-erasing fabric marker. Before you begin to sew, you need to mark the position of the buttonholes on the fabric. Measure the diameter of the button using your buttonhole foot or your hand gauge.

For both options, do a test on a separate piece of fabric. It makes sense to do the test on material that is the same as your work.

Only then can you be sure that the settings on the sewing machine suit the properties of the fabric and will create a neat buttonhole.

You have to be a little careful when working close to seams, e.g., the top button on the boiled wool jacket or suit. At this juncture, many machines encounter considerable difficulties. If necessary, you can always switch to manually sewing the buttonhole.

## MANUALLY SEWING BUTTONHOLES

Of course, manually sewn buttonholes look good and are also functional. When modern technology has reached its limit, it is useful to be able to manually sew a buttonhole. It is a good idea to know and be able to use a couple of settings. As a rule of thumb, the more carefully and slowly you work, the better the result.

## SEWING BUTTONHOLES USING A BUTTONHOLE FOOT

Today, nearly all conventional sewing machines come with a buttonhole system. This system includes a buttonhole foot, which you use to determine the size required and to partially or fully sew the buttonhole (depending on the machine).

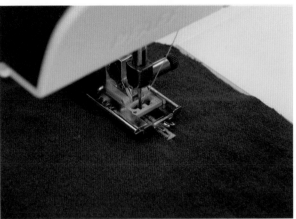

1. Set your machine to a wide zig-zag stitch with a stitch length of zero and start at the top of the buttonhole with 5 to 6 stitches (securing at the top). Finish with the needle where you started.

2. Now change your stitch to a very small and narrow zig-zag stitch with a stitch length of 0.25 mm and width of 2 mm. Sew one side of the buttonhole along the marking.

1. Now change back to the wide zig-zag stitch and repeat step 1 with the last stitches (securing at the bottom). The needle should now be stuck in the fabric.

2. Using the small stitch setting from step 2, sew backwards to where you started. Don't forget to secure in the ends. Cut the hole. Done!

1. Once the buttonholes have been marked on the fabric, sew them according to the instructions for your sewing machine using the appropriate buttonhole setting.

**TIP:**
*Use a seam ripper to carefully cut the buttonhole at the end.*

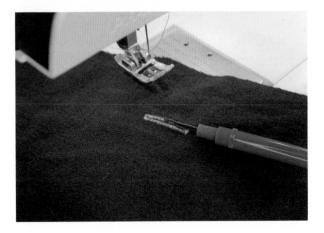

# NEATLY ATTACHING CUFFS BETWEEN LAYERS

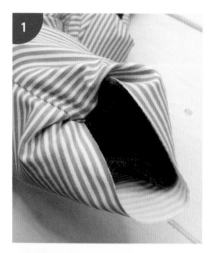
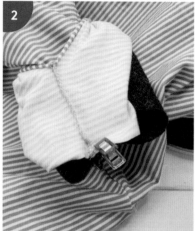

1.  The principle of this technique is sewing the garment with wrong sides together and then turning so that the right side is facing out. Sew the cuff fabric with right sides together to form a circle. Then fold it in half so that the wrong sides are now together – this is how it will be sewn into the jacket or playsuit. Pin the sleeve seams on top of each other, so that now the wrong sides are together. "Reach through the opening on the sleeve and pull the end of the sleeve through it."

2.  Now place seams with right sides together and pin in place.

3.  Place the cuff with its seam directly between the outer material and the lining (raw end of the cuff to the sleeve end). All seams of the four touching layers (lining, cuff, cuff, outer material) are positioned over each other.

4.  Sew completely around the sleeve hem once. It is fiddly but doable.

5.  You now have a neat cuff that should look like this on the inside.

# HEMS

Hems lend all garments a neat finish and are therefore essential for all projects. Here is a selection of hems that will give your project a beautiful finish. You can choose different types of hems depending on whether you are working with an overlocker or not and upon the fabric used.

### Simple hem

The simple hem is finished along the raw edge, folded approximately 1 cm inwards and sewn in place using a straight stitch.

### Double turned hem

With this kind of hem, no cut raw edges are visible because the edge is turned in twice and sewn in place. It is the most common type of hem, and it gives the garment a very high-end appearance because everything has been neatly sewn in.

### Turn-up hem

The turn-up hem is a current fashion trend and is used as a very casual hem primarily with French terry or jersey fabric.

Instead of simply turning the sewn edge in, you fold it out twice and hold it in place either by sewing around the hem or only where the open edges meet.

### Geraffter Saum

Thanks to its loose and airy qualities, muslin is particularly well suited for ruffling. A tunnel with elastic threaded through gives hems on sleaves and legs a pretty finish and also a cute look.

**TIP:**

*It is normally good to have an iron to hand when sewing hems (with the exception of muslin).*

# PROJECTS

# LET'S GET STARTED

## THE CUTTING PATTERN

The cutting patterns in this book are located on the accompanying pattern sheets.

The different sizes are shown with different outlines.

To trace them use transparent paper (tissue paper) or special pattern paper and a marker. Once you have decided on a suitable size, trace its outline and do not forget to add the markings.

> **TIP:**
>
> *Always label your pattern pieces with the name of the pattern, the size and all other information, such as markings, seam allowance, hem allowance, etc. In this way, you will later be able to find everything quickly and easily.*
>
> *Think up a good filing system. My cut patterns are sorted according to model and size and hang in a hanging folder. A good system means that you always have your cut patterns sorted according to size and easily accessible.*

## THE CUT

At the start of every project, there is a list of all the required pattern pieces and the seam allowances.

1. Pin the cut pattern to the fabric in line with the run of the thread.
   Run of the thread means parallel to the two self-finished sides (selvedge).

2. Use dressmaking scissors or a rotary cutter to cut out the pieces.

3. Trace all markings on to the fabric.

## CUTTING ON THE FOLD

You can cut front and back pieces on the fold. To do so, fold the fabric in line with the run of the thread so that right sides are facing. Then position the cut pattern with the label "fold" directly over the fold in the fabric (fold). Important: there is no seam allowance on the fold.

Mirrored pieces, e.g., sleeves, are cut from a double layer of fabric. To do so, fold the fabric along the run of the thread. In this case, the cut pattern is not positioned on the fold, but more centrally in the fabric leaving the seam allowance. Two pattern pieces are cut out. In the rest of the book, I call this "mirrored".

## SEAM ALLOWANCE

The seam allowance is the area between the seam and the raw edge.

For all projects in this book, I recommend a seam allowance of 0.75 cm.

Above all with woven fabric, observing the seam allowance is of great importance. Many cotton or linen fabrics fray badly, which means the seam allowance is very important so that the stitches do not fall out later. The seam allowance is also important to allow the sewing machine foot to be easily used. There are lines on your sewing machine for better orientation when observing seam allowances.

All cut pattern pieces are WITHOUT the seam allowance.

## HEM ALLOWANCE

A hem allowance is always needed where there is a raw edge on the garment.

You must always plan it for sleeves, bottom edges and sometimes on necklines. The exact measurement of the hem allowance will be given separately for each project.

If you choose a different type of hem to the one described for the project, then you must adapt the hem allowance to suit your chosen hem.

Please pay close attention to the specific information in the project descriptions.

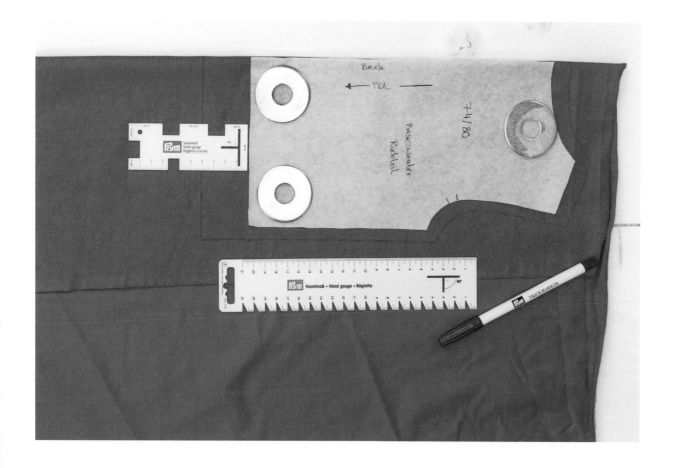

# THE PROJECTS

I love the minimalistic Scandi look.

Simple cuts, muted colours and fairly-produced fabrics are the heart of the patterns. They are reduced to the bare essentials, authentic, comfortable and at the same time practical for growing children in our far too fast-paced world. We don't need much, but we should love and value what we have, and that includes our clothing.

## DUAL SIZING

50/56 (0 to 3/6 months) ◉
62/68 (3/6 to 6/9 months) ◉
74/80 (9/12 to 12/18 months) ◉
86/92 (18/24 months to 2/3 years) ◉
98/104 (3/4 to 4/5 years) ◉

## LEVEL OF DIFFICULTY

◉ Easy-peasy!

◉ ◉ Take your time and enjoy a relaxing warm drink while working!

◉ ◉ ◉ Spend some time and effort for wonderful results!

### FINDING THE RIGHT DUAL SIZE

I consciously decided to design the patterns in this book using dual sizing. From my own experience, I know the amount of time, effort and passion that goes into every item of handmade clothing. Therefore, the joy is doubled when it fits the child for longer and can be worn frequently.

Part of my philosophy is that your little one and you, as a creative mother, should get joy from your creation for as long as possible. Also, in regard to thinking sustainably, it is important for me that clothes can grow with the child. With a little skill, you can also adapt each size in one or the other direction and in that way get a perfect result.

Essentially, almost all designs are generously sized and designed to grow with your child - your child's body length is a good guide to determine the right size.

If your little one is exactly between two sizes, then you can adapt the cut using the seam allowance.

**For example:** If your child is closer to a 92 than an 86. Simply add a little extra to the seam allowance which will automatically make the pattern bigger. In the opposite case, simply leave out the seam allowance and then you are closer to an 86 and have shrunk that pattern.

**TIP:**

*Each project includes information about the amount of fabric required. It has been calculated based on the usual fabric width of 140 cm.*

*Remember that woven fabric shrinks after washing.*

# PROJECTS

## SPRING
## SUMMER

# BLOOMERS

**LEVEL OF DIFFICULTY:**
◉ Easy-peasy

*Bloomers are a great all-rounder in a tot's wardrobe. Comfortable, practical and super cute, your little one can wear these bloomers the whole year through. In summer, bloomers can hide nappies and they look great in winter combined with tights or leggings and warm boots. They make everyone smile, boys and girls alike.*

## FABRIC:

Muslin, linen, cord, rib knit, seersucker, waffle cotton and much more.

Linen mix was used in the pattern instructions. The mini model is wearing bloomers made of muslin with a paper bag waist.

## YOU NEED:

**Fabric:**
● **Size 50-68:** 30 cm
  **Size 70-104:** 40 cm
● 2 cm wide elastic for waistband,
  1 cm wide elastic for leg hem
● Safety pin

## CUTTING:

Add a seam allowance of 0.75 cm all the way round.

● 1 x waistband cut on the fold (sheet 2)
● 1 x front piece cut on the fold (sheet 2)
● 1 x back piece cut on the fold (sheet 2)

Elastic in correct length for waistband and legs

| Size | Waist | Leg |
|------|-------|------|
| 50/56 | 34 cm | 18 cm |
| 62/68 | 39 cm | 20 cm |
| 74/80 | 42 cm | 21.5 cm |
| 86/92 | 46 cm | 23 cm |
| 98/104 | 48 cm | 24.5 cm |

(All measurements are intended as a guide; it is best to measure and try on your child.)

> **TIP:**
> *You can create a cute paper bag waistband by doubling the height of the waistband strip and finishing it off with an additional seam above the elastic to create a tunnel.*

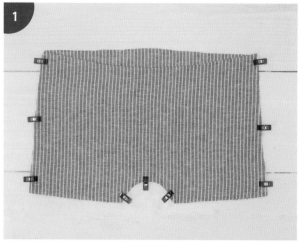

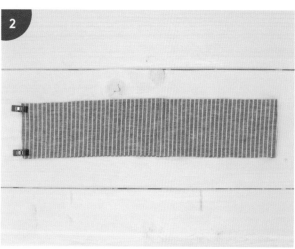

1. Position the pattern pieces for the front and back piece so that the right sides are facing. First pin the two pieces together and use straight stitch or overlock stitch to sew together both sides and the crotch seam.

2. Now it is time for the bloomers' waistband: sew the two short edges together with the right sides together.

3. Now you should have a ring, which has the same circumference as the bloomers. Fold it in half lengthways with wrong sides together(depending on the material, you made need to iron it).

Turn the shorts so that the right side is facing out. Pin and then sew the waistband to the top edge of the shorts with right sides together. So that you will be able to add the elastic, leave an opening of approximately 4 cm.

4. Now pull elastic measuring the correct length (it is best to try it on your child) through the opening in waistband. With a seam allowance of 1 cm, sew in the ends of the elastic together using a stretch stitch. Ensure that the elastic is correctly positioned in the waistband and does not become twisted.

**BLOOMERS**

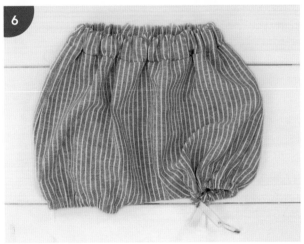

5. Then sew closed the opening on the waistband. So that the elastic does not get twisted later through wear and washing, I fix it in place from the outside with a few stitches in the side seams of the waistband.

6. Now for the leg hems. For the cute bloomers look we need to use elastic again. Finish both edges with overlock or zigzag stitch. Fold or iron (depending on the fabric) both leg hems 1.5 cm inwards, pin it all securely in place and sew the tunnel that has been formed in the seam allowance of the hem edge. For both legs, you will leave an opening for the elastic.

Ensure that these openings are at the back of the bloomers because you will need to stitch the openings closed later. Now pull the thin elastic (again it is also best to measure on your child because there can be vast variations in size around the thigh) through the two tunnels. Sew the ends of each piece of elastic together and sew both openings closed.

7. Now the super sweet bloomers are finished!

# MUSLIN SHIRT

**LEVEL OF DIFFICULTY:**
◉ Easy-peasy

*The muslin shirt is based on a cool, relaxed cut and is perfect for hot days in spring and summer. It combines the great properties of muslin with a simple-to-make and comfortable design for every day wear. The neck ensures that you can get the head of even the wildest, most stubborn child through it. Muslin also keeps little hot heads cool.*

**FABRIC:**

Muslin, but also jersey etc.

Muslin and cuffing fabric were used for the example in the instructions.

**YOU NEED:**

Fabric:
◉ **Sizes 50-68:** 40 cm
  **Sizes 74-104:** 50 cm
◉ Cuffing fabric for the neck
  **Sizes 50-104:** 5 cm

**CUTTING:**

Add a seam allowance of 0.75 cm all the way round.

Hem allowance on arms
4 cm (when cutting pay attention that the seam allowance does not become thinner as the sleeve piece is folded up on the outside)

Hem allowance bottom
3 cm (depending on desired length)

Main fabric:
◉ 1 x front piece cut on the fold (sheet 1)
◉ 1 x back piece cut on the fold (sheet 1)

Cuffing fabric:
◉ 1 x neck cut on the fold (sheet 1)

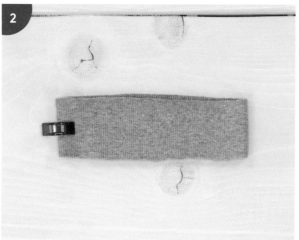

1. Place the front and back pieces on top of each other with right sides together. Pin and then sew the two pieces together on the shoulders and the sides.

2. Sew the two short ends of the neck strip together to form a ring with the right sides together.

3. Turn the ring so that the wrong side is now facing in and pin it on to the neckline so that both right sides are together. Now sew in place using the overlocker or zigzag stitch on the sewing machine. In doing so, position the neck seam in line with the shoulder seam so that when the shirt is finished, there will be a beautiful continuous seam in the neck area.

4. Finish the arms and the bottom of the shirt.

5. Now select a hem from the types of hems explained at the start of the book. For the sleeves, I used the turn-up hem. It is simple to work, and it creates a cool look. For the turn-up hem, you fold the finished sleeves over and outwards twice by approximately 1 cm and then sew the folds in place along the side seams using a short straight stitch.

6. At the bottom, I simply folded the finished edge over twice and sewed it in place with a straight stitch. However, there is no limit to your creativity with this shirt.

# MUSLIN SWEATER

**LEVEL OF DIFFICULTY:**
⊛ Easy-peasy

*This sweater is a great all-rounder that can be made with many types of fabric. It is particularly airy and loose when made of muslin and is therefore perfect for warm days. The waistband ensures it fits comfortably and the long cuffs on the sleeves allow it to grow with your child. Use this pattern to sew the most beautiful creations, not just from muslin.*

**FABRIC:**
Muslin, but also rib knit etc.

Muslin was used for the example in the instructions.

**YOU NEED:**

Fabric:
⊛ **Sizes 50-68:** 30 cm
  **Sizes 74-104:** 45 cm
⊛ Cuffing fabric for the neck, waist and sleeves:

**Sizes 50-68:** 30 cm
**Sizes 74-104:** 45 cm

**CUTTING:**
Add a seam allowance of 0.75 cm all the way round.

Muslin:
⊛ 1 x front piece cut on the fold (sheet 1)
⊛ 1 x back piece cut on the fold (sheet 1)
⊛ 2 x sleeves (mirrored) (sheet 1)

Cuffing fabric:
⊛ 1 x neckline piece cut on the fold (sheet 1)
⊛ 1 x waistband cut on the fold (sheet 1)
⊛ 2 x sleeve cuffs cut on the fold (sheet 1)

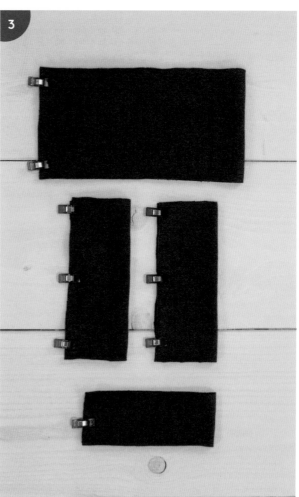

1. Place the front and back on top of each other with right sides together. Pin and then sew the two pieces together at the shoulders and the sides.

2. Now place the joined two pieces in front of you with the right sides facing up. Using the markings on the cut pattern as a guide, pin both the sleeves into the armholes and sew in place.

3. Sew all four cuff strips for the neck, waist and the two sleeves.

4. Sew the side seams of the sleeves, then turn the sweater so that the right side faces out.

5.  Turn all cuffs so that the wrong side is facing in. Pin them to the neck, the bottom of the sweater and the sleeves so that the right sides of the cuffs are facing the right side of the sweater. Machine sew in place using the zigzag stitch or use the overlocker. Always place the seam on the neck cuff in line with the side seam so that when the sweater is finished, there will be a beautiful continuous seam in the neck area.

6.  Your muslin sweater is now finished!

# ROMPER

## LEVEL OF DIFFICULTY:

◉ ◉ Take your time and enjoy a relaxing warm drink while working!

*Whether made from linen, muslin, seersucker or other kinds of cotton fabric, your little one will look picture perfect in this sweet romper suit. Whether you combine it with bare legs in the summer or tights in the autumn, it is suitable to be worn the whole year through. It is a really easy pattern, which calls for a little experience in a couple of places. Have faith in yourself, and the results are guaranteed to be cute.*

## FABRIC:

Muslin, linen, cord, waffle cotton and many other cotton fabrics, as well as elastic fabrics, such as jersey, French terry and rib knit.

Striped cotton was used for the example in the instructions.

## YOU NEED:

### Fabric:

● **Sizes 50-68:** 55 cm

   **Sizes 74-104:** 65 cm

● 2 cm wide elastic for the back trousers' waistband

● 1 cm wide elastic for the leg holes

● H200 vilene interfacing

● 1 piece of elastic in the required length

● 2 buttons

## CUTTING:

Add a seam allowance of 0.75 cm all the way round.

● 2 x front pieces cut on the fold (sheet 4)

● 1 x back piece cut on the fold (sheet 4)

● 1 x back piece for waistband cut on the fold (sheet 4)

● 1 x piece of elastic in the required length

● 2 x buttons

● 2 x straps (sheet 4)

### Length of the elastic

| Size | Back of waist | Leg |
|------|---------------|------|
| 50/56 | 25 cm | 22 cm |
| 62/68 | 30 cm | 26 cm |
| 74/80 | 33 cm | 28 cm |
| 86/92 | 36 cm | 30 cm |
| 98/104 | 38 cm | 31 cm |

(All measurements are intended as a guide; it is best to measure and try on your child.)

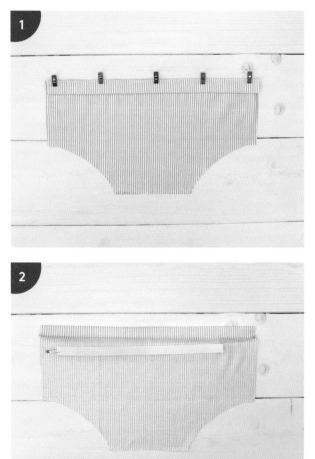

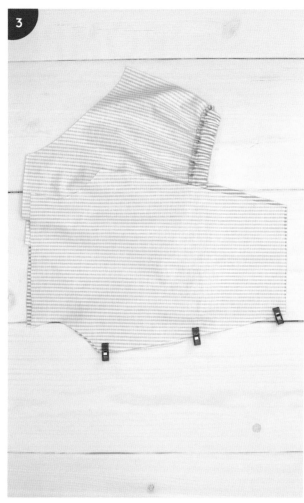

1. Fold or iron the waistband strip for the back of the shorts lengthways. Pin it to the top of the shorts right sides together and use an overlocker or sewing machine to sew in place with stitches along the top raw edges.

2. Now thread the wider length of elastic through the waistband. To do so, hold it in place with a short straight stitch on the raw edge on one side of the shorts, then continue pulling it through and fix in place in the same manner on the other side. The back piece should now have the typical, ruffled, romper look. You can achieve a high-end appearance, if you stitch the waistband from the outside close to the edge.

3. This part is a little tricky and the correct position of the layers is crucial. Take one of the two front pieces, and position it with the right side facing up in front of you (when finished it will be the visible front of the romper). Then take the ruffled shorts and pin them with right sides together on to the front piece (the crotch seams should lie over each other). Now place the second front piece with the wrong side facing up on top of them as the final layer. The second front piece is now positioned right sides together with the first front piece, and with its right side facing the wrong side of the ruffled trousers.

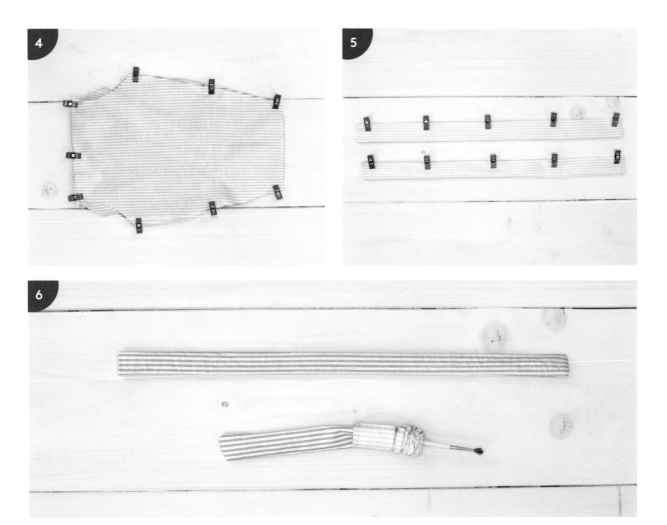

4. When everything has been pinned and the layers lie neatly over each other, sew the two side seams and the crotch seam. When doing so, pay particular attention to the two places where the elastic is. I always give these places an additional seam, so that everything really is secure.

5. In the next step, you will make the two straps. On each strap iron on a strip of H200 interfacing on the wrong side so that it covers half of the strap. It will give the straps some firmness and strengthen the buttonholes. Iron or fold the two straps lengthways with right sides together and pin them. Stitch along the long side and one of the two short edges.

6. After you have turned the straps so the right sides face out, you can use the straps (there are special tools for turning, however, wooden paint brushes or wooden spoons are just as good).

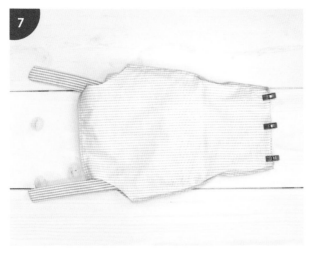

7. Now pin the straps inside the top edge of the romper, which is still raw. This is where the straps with the right side out meet the still unsewn top of the romper. Now pin the two pieces of the romper together with the straps and sew. I add an additional seam over the straps so that everything is secure.

8. Now pull everything through one of the still unsewn leg holes so that the right sides are facing out. Position the leg holes so that the layers of each one lie neatly over each other (remember, there are two front pieces) and finish them using an overlocker or zigzag stitch.

9. Make a small tunnel of approximately 1.5 cm in width by turning the leg seam in on itself and then sew close to the finished edge. Leave a small hole in each leg so that you can thread the elastic through.

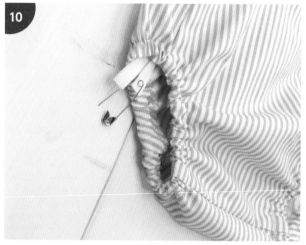

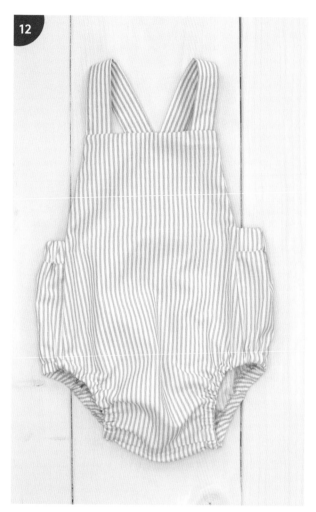

10. Thread the two pieces of elastic through the legs and sew together using stretch stitch and then sew up the openings.

11. Now you are almost done. It is best to work out the best position for the buttonholes by measuring directly on your child. Sew the buttonholes (you can have one or two on each strap so that the romper can grow with the child) and then attach two matching buttons to the waistband.

12. If you simply can't wait to see the romper on your child, simply use vario pliers and press studs.

TIP:
*There is a on page 76 for how to finish your romper with cute knots instead of buttons.*

# SHIRT WITH BUTTON PLACKET

**LEVEL OF DIFFICULTY:**
◉ ◉ Take your time and enjoy a relaxing warm drink while working!

*This shirt is based on an uncomplicated pattern without much fuss. Thanks to its floaty-casual fit, it is perfect for spring and summer. The side button placket makes it easy to put on and take off and the long sleeves are great for protecting young arms from the sun. Summer, sun and sea, here we come!*

**FABRIC:**

Muslin, linen, seersucker and soft draping cotton fabric.

Muslin was used for the example in the instructions.

**YOU NEED:**

Fabric:
● **Sizes 50-68:** 50 cm
  **Sizes 74-104:** 65 cm
● Two buttons or press studs
● H250 vilene interfacing

**CUTTING:**

Add a seam allowance of 0.75 cm all the way round.
● 1 x front piece cut on the fold (sheet 4)
● 1 x back piece cut on the fold (sheet 4)
● 2 x sleeves (mirrored) (sheet 4)

Hem allowance on neck
1,5 cm

Hem allowance on sleeves
2 cm

Hem allowance bottom
2 cm

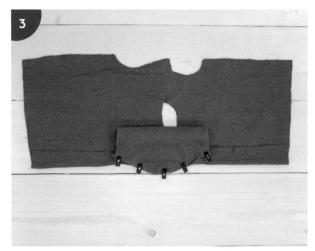

1. Place the front and back piece over each other with right sides together and pin the "simple" shoulder seam. Sew this seam together.

2. Cut two thin strips of H250 interfacing and iron them on to the second shoulder on the wrong side of the fabric.

3. We are starting with the "simple" sleeve. Place the piece with the right side facing up in front of you and position the first sleeve in the armhole according to the markings and sew the pieces together.

4. Finish the neck. Then fold it over twice and sew in place close to the edge.

**SHIRT WITH BUTTON PLACKET**

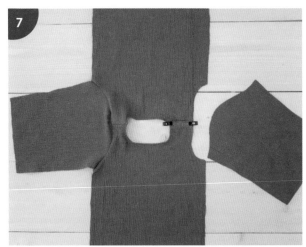

5. Fold the button placket according to the instructions on the pattern sheet (twice for the back of shoulder, once for the front of shoulder) and sew close to the edge.

6. If you want to make the shirt with buttons, now sew the button holes (tips on how to do so can be found on page 26). Alternatively, you can also use press studs.

7. Now, we will work on the second sleeve. It is important that you place the parts of the button placket carefully over each other and secure in place. The side with buttonholes should be on the top. Once again position the sleeve in the armholes according to the markings on the pattern sheet and sew into place.

8. Sew together the seams on the bottom of the sleeves and the two sides of the shirt.

9.  Finish the sleeve seams and the bottom of the shirt using an overlocker or zigzag stitch on the sewing machine.

10. Sew the hems on the sleeves and the bottom of the shirt in the same way as you did for the neck but make them a little wider: fold them over twice and sew in place close to the edge and ta-dah! To finish, sew the buttons in place on the shoulder.

# OVERALL

### LEVEL OF DIFFICULTY:

◉ ◉ Take your time and enjoy a relaxing warm drink while working!

*The overall is an uncomplicated onesie in a serene Scandinavian style. The pattern is relaxed and airy and the long button placket makes putting it on and taking it off child's play. Small details, such as sleeve seams, can be sewn differently so that the overall does not just suit baby girls, but can also see little rascals through the summer. You can make it with long or short sleeves.*

### FABRIC:

Muslin, linen, and soft draping cotton fabric.

Soft organic muslin was used for the example in the instructions.

### YOU NEED:

Fabric:
- **Sizes 50-68:** 60 cm
  **Sizes 74-80:** 70 cm
  **Sizes 86-104:** 95 cm
- Three buttons, alternatively press studs
- H250 vilene interfacing

### CUTTING:

Add a seam allowance of 0.75 cm.
- 1 x front piece cut on the fold (sheet 2)
- 1 x back piece cut on the fold (sheet 2)
- 2 x sleeves (mirrored) (sheet 2)
- 2 x button plackets (mirrored) (sheet 2)

Hem allowance neck
1.5 cm

Hem allowance on sleeves
2 cm

Hem allowance on legs
2 cm

Hem allowance on button placket
Top and bottom 2 cm

> **TIP:**
> *The button placket is created by cutting down the centre of the front piece according to the length drawn on the pattern sheet (see step 1 of the instructions).*

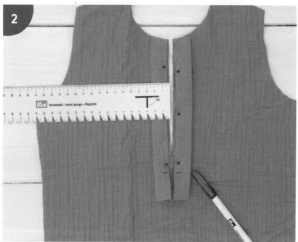

1. While cutting out, you will create the opening for the button placket by just cutting down the centre of the front piece. Strengthen the pattern pieces of the button placket with a strip of H250 interfacing.

2. Now work on the right side of the front piece. Fold the button placket pieces so that wrong sides are together and pin them in place along the raw edge of the front piece. Both pieces of the button placket should be 0.5 cm from the raw edge, use the hand gauge to measure the distance. Use the self-erasing marker to make a mark 2 cm below the end of the cut on both parts of the button placket. Sew the button placket to the raw edge, i.e., along the pins down to the lower marking.

3. You should still be working on the right side of the front piece. Now, starting from the centre of the opening, cut towards each of the marked ends of the seam for the two parts of the button placket creating a wedge.

4. Now carefully open the button placket from the back and place the pieces carefully over each other. No creases should form on the front piece.

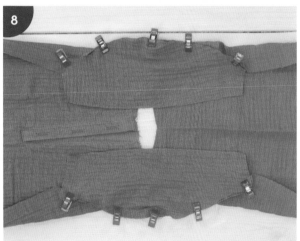

5. When you fold up the lower part of the overall, it should look like the photo. Secure all three layers with a seam along the pins as indicated in the photo. Trim the button placket and finish it using an overlocker or zigzag stitch on a sewing machine (which I prefer in this case).

6. Sew three buttonholes on the button placket piece that is positioned on the top. You should have marked their position with the self-erasing marker or pins when cutting out.

7. Now place the back and the front piece with right sides together. Sew both parts together along the shoulder seams.

8. Position the sleeves on the arm holes with right sides together and sew in place.

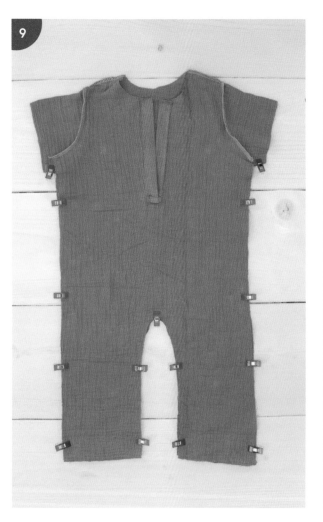

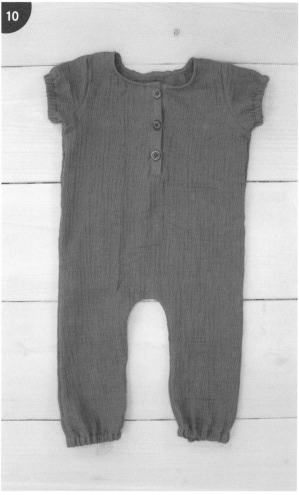

9. Then sew the two sides and the crotch together. If you use an overlocker, do not forget to secure the crotch and the sleeves with an additional seam using the sewing machine.

10. Finish the raw edges on the sleeves and legs and decide on the type of hem. For the example, I used a ruffled version with elastic. For the ruffled hem, fold the muslin approximately 1.5 cm inwards and secure the fabric with stitches. Leave a hole of about 3 cm in order to thread the elastic through. Pull the elastic through the tunnel and sew the ends of the elastic together and then close the holes.

# DUNGAREES

**LEVEL OF DIFFICULTY:**
◉ ◉ Take your time and enjoy a relaxing warm drink while working!

*Traditional dungarees are celebrating their comeback. The on-trend design and the details on the back make these trousers a total eye-catcher. The straps can be individually tailored to your little one by positioning the buttonholes or by using the knotting option. Soft elastic at the back ensures a perfect fit. The pattern is really uncomplicated and very versatile. Adapt into shorts, pinafore or with dungarees with a waistband – everything is possible.*

## FABRIC:
Muslin, linen and many other cotton weaves, but also elastic fabrics, such as jersey, French terry or rib knit (but then without seam allowance)

Organic cotton was used, and turn-up hems were added for the example in the instructions.

## YOU NEED:
**Fabric:**
- **Sizes 50-68:** 55 cm
  **Sizes 74-86:** 65 cm
  **Sizes 86-104:** 85 cm
- 2cm wide length of elastic for the back of the waistband
- H200 vilene interfacing
- 2 buttons, alternatively press studs
- **Optional:** cuffing fabric for the leg ends (for this option, you need to shorten the long legs by the length of the cuff)

## CUTTING:
Add a seam allowance of 0.75 cm all the way round.
- 1 x front piece cut on the fold (sheet 2)
- 1 x front piece lining cut on the fold (sheet 2)
- 1 x back piece cut on the fold (sheet 2)
- 1 x waistband for the back cut on the fold (sheet 2)
- 2 x straps (sheet 2)
- 1 x piece of elastic in the required length (approximately, 2/3 of the waistband)

**Cuffing fabric:**
For the option with cuffs: 2 x leg cuff (sheet 2)

**Hem allowance bottom**
Add a seam allowance of 2 cm to the legs (long and short designs)

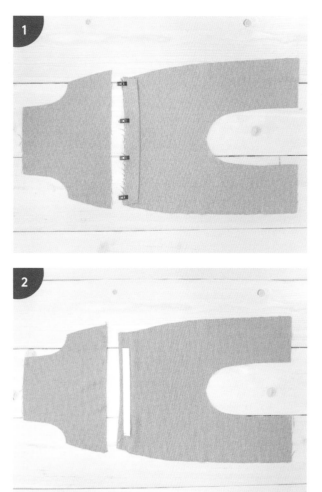

1. Fold or iron the waistband for the back piece in half lengthways. Pin it to the upper edge of the trousers and sew in place with your sewing machine or overlocker. Finish the bottom end of the lining as well.

2. Now thread the elastic through the waistband and secure it with short straight stitches first on one side of the trousers, then continue threading it through and secure on the other side in the same way. Now the back piece has the typical ruffled look of dungarees.

3. Now, with right sides together sew the lining to the top of the front piece along the sides of the bib.

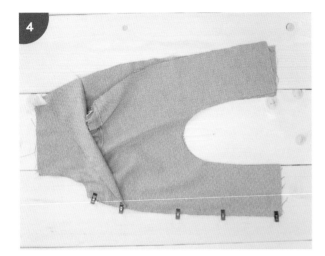

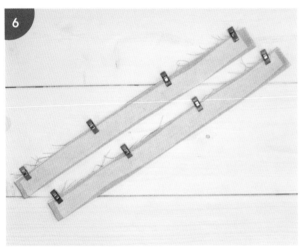

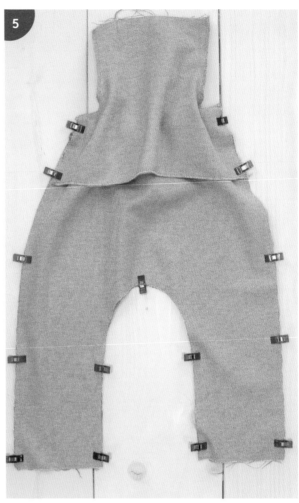

4. This part is a little tricky and the correct position of the layers is crucial. Position the front piece of the trousers with the sewn-on lining in front of you. Fold up the lining so that the ruffled back of the trousers can be placed on the front piece of the trousers with right sides together (the crotch seams are flush). Then fold the lining back down.

5. Once everything has been securely pinned and the layers are neatly on top of each other, sew the two side seams and the crotch seam. Pay particular attention to the two places where the elastic is. I always give these places an additional seam, so that everything is really secure.

6. In the next step, you will make the two straps. Iron a strip of H200 interfacing on to each strap so that it covers half of the strap on the wrong side. It will make the straps firmer and strengthen the buttonholes. Iron or fold the two straps lengthways with right sides together and pin them. Now stitch along the long side and one of the two short edges.

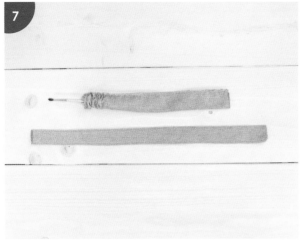

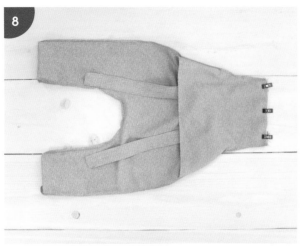

7. After you have turned the straps so the right sides face out, you can use the straps (there are special tools for turning, however, conventional wooden brushes or wooden spoons are just as good).

8. Now pin the straps inside the top edge of the dungarees, which is still raw. This is where the open short edge of the straps with the right side out meets the unsewn top of the dungarees. Now pin the two pieces of the dungarees with the straps and sew. I add an additional seam over the straps so that everything is secure. Now you can turn the trousers the right way out.

9. It is best to try out the best position for the buttonholes directly on your child. Work the buttonholes (you can have one or two on each strap so that the dungarees can grow with the child) and then attach two matching buttons to the waistband. You also have the option to knot the straps; instructions are in the mini-tutorial on the next pages.

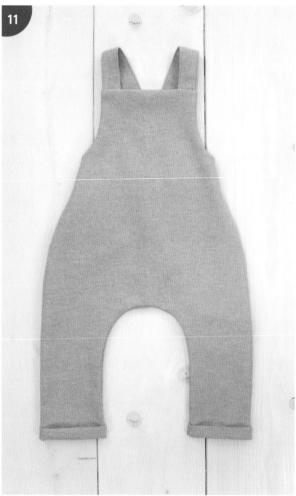

10. Finally finish the ends of the legs using an overlocker or zigzag stitch on a sewing machine. For smooth fabric like in the photos, I prefer the turn up hem. It gives the dungarees a special look.

11. Now these stylish dungarees are ready for your little one!

**TIP:**
*You can quickly turn these dungarees into a cute pinafore. Simply use the markings for the short design and cut over the crotch seam in a curve towards the fold.*

## KNOT DESIGN FOR DUNGAREES AND ROMPER SUIT

An alternative to straps with buttons for dungarees and rompers suits is a cute design with knots. The buttonholes are made in the back waistband and then the straps are simply crossed over and pulled through the holes. The knot can be used to individually adapt the length of the straps and the garment grows with your child. However, this design is only recommended for the larger sizes that are worn by children who can already walk. It is not comfortable for little ones to lie on the knots.

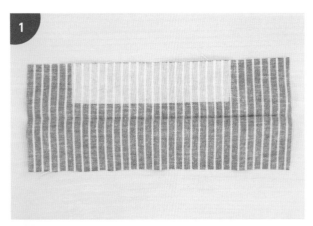

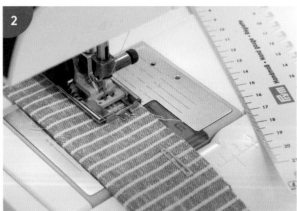

1. For this design, you do not iron the interfacing on to the straps but instead on to the central area of the waistband for the trousers.

2. Before you sew the trousers together, sew two buttonholes with a length of approximately 18 mm at a distance of approximately 5 cm from each other.

3. Continue with the project instructions as normal.

**TIP:**
*You can get a classic little girl look by knotting the straps into a cute little bow.*

# BABY HAT

**LEVEL OF DIFFICULTY:**
◉ Easy-peasy

*This easy to sew pointed baby hat turns your little one into a real cutie-pie. Both muslin and this hat shape are experiencing a comeback. Light-weight muslin makes this hat perfect for spring and summer, and it has a very comfortable fit, above all in the first months.*

**FABRIC:**
Muslin (thin jersey is also well suited as the lining material)

**YOU NEED:**
Fabric:
◉ **Head circumference 36-44:** 30 cm
  **Head circumference 44-52:** 35 cm
◉ Hat straps made of muslin or thin jersey, length approximately 60-70 cm

**CUTTING:**
Add a seam allowance of 0.75 cm all the way round.

◉ 4 x hat pieces (mirrored, 2 each from outer material and lining) (sheet 3)

Hem allowance
Add 3 cm to bottom for the tunnel.

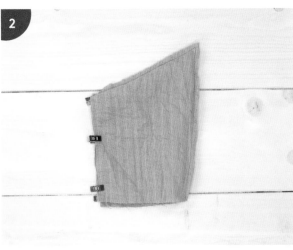

1. Place two hat parts cut from the same fabric over each other and finish along the edges marked with the clips. I sew this hat using the normal sewing machine, so the seam can be neatly folded apart and won't press into the baby's head or get in the way. Trim the tip on each piece (inside the seam allowance) so that you can neatly push out the tip when the hat is turned. Do the same for the other two hat parts.

2. Now place the two created hats inside each other with right sides together and sew the front seam marked with clips.

3. Now turn the hat so that wrong sides are together and then sew the most recently sewn seam neatly on the right side.

4. Finish the lower raw edge using the zigzag stitch on your sewing machine.

**BABY HAT**

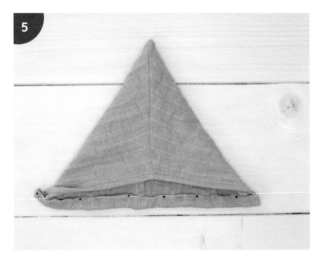

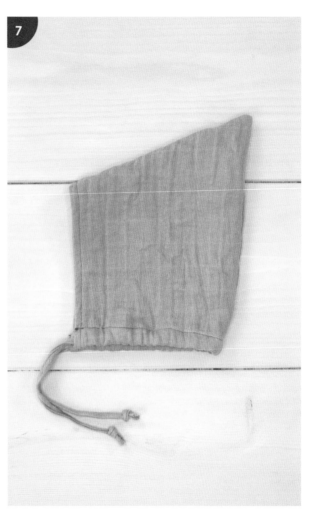

5. Now sew the tunnel for the straps. To do so, fold in the bottom edge. I have marked the tunnel here with pins because in the same step the still visible zigzag stitch will be folded in and sewn up. Use a straight stitch to sew the tunnel.

6. Now make the strap from muslin. Cut a strip approximately 3 cm wide and 60 cm long. Now fold in 0.5 cm on both sides and then fold the strip in half lengthways. Stitch along the whole length. A thinly cut jersey strip is also a pretty and simple alternative.

7. Now thread the strap through the tunnel and voilà, your beautiful hat is ready to wear.

# MUSLIN SLEEPING BAG

### LEVEL OF DIFFICULTY:

◉ ◉ Take your time and enjoy a relaxing warm drink while working!

*This muslin sleeping bag is a perfect companion from spring to autumn. Its dual layers give it a great appearance and it should not be missing from any nursery. Although the pattern may be a little tricky in a few places, you will be rewarded with a beautiful result.*

### FABRIC:

Muslin

This pattern is also suitable for other fabrics, so you can use it to create a sleeping bag for the colder seasons too.

### YOU NEED:

Fabric:

● **Sizes 50-68:** 160 cm

  **Sizes 74-104:** 200 cm

● H250 vilene interfacing

● Press studs, alternatively also wooden buttons

● Vario pliers

### CUTTING:

Add a seam allowance of 0.75 cm all the way round.

Outer material:

2 x front pieces (mirrored) (sheet 1 and sheet 2)

1 x back piece cut on the fold (sheet 3 and sheet 4)

Inner material:

2 x front pieces (mirrored) (sheet 1 and sheet 2)

1 x back piece cut on the fold (sheet 3 and sheet 4)

Hem allowance

2 cm for the shoulder seams

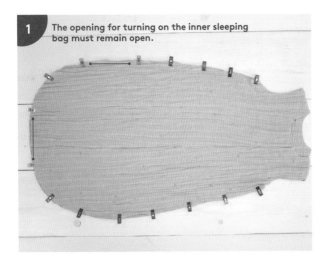

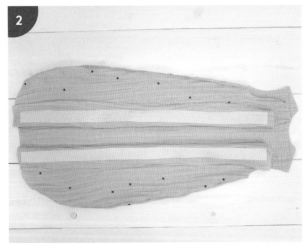

**1** The opening for turning on the inner sleeping bag must remain open.

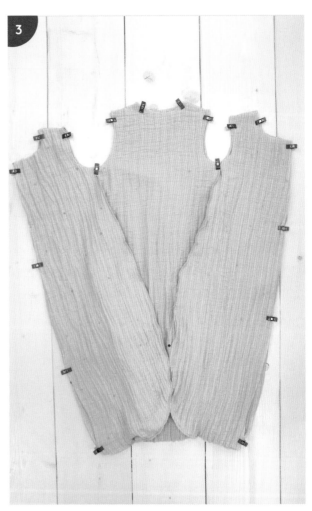

1. In the first step, sew an inner and an outer sleeping bag. Leave unsewn both the shoulder seams and a strip in the lower area, where the button plackets shall be. Leave an approximately 10 cm opening for turning in the side seam of the inner sleeping bag. Sew both pieces according to the markings.

2. Iron two strips of H250 interfacing on the wrong side of one of the sleeping bags where the button placket will be. It will enable the press studs to be securely attached there.

3. Now put the sleeping bags inside of each other with right sides together. This requires a little patience and skill. Do not get confused by the many layers and ensure that the sleeping bag with the opening for turning is positioned as the sleeping bag on the inside. Sew sleeping bags together along the button placket, then around the neck, the back and the armholes.

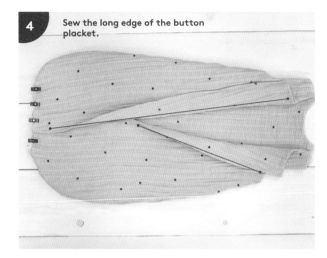

**4.** Sew the long edge of the button placket.

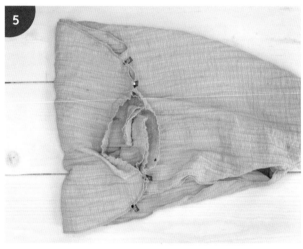

5

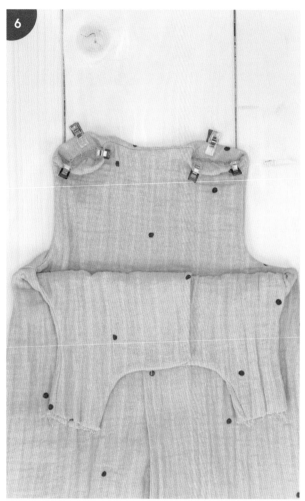

6

4. Turn the sleeping bag so that right sides are facing out. The parts of the button placket should be at the front and positioned over each other. Then stitch close to the edges (I prefer to leave the width of a presser foot, but it is a matter of taste) around the button placket. Stop at the neckline. Secure the raw opening from the outside using clips.

5. Now put your hand in the opening for turning and pull this clipped opening out of the sleeping bag. Undo the clips, however when doing so hold the layers together in the same way as you had secured them from the outside.

It is important that the upper and lower flap are positioned over each other and do not form any folds. Now carefully sew all the layers together here.

6. Once again turn the sleeping bag so that right sides are facing out. In order to sew the shoulders, fold the two open "shoulder rings" of the back piece approximately 2-3 cm inwards.

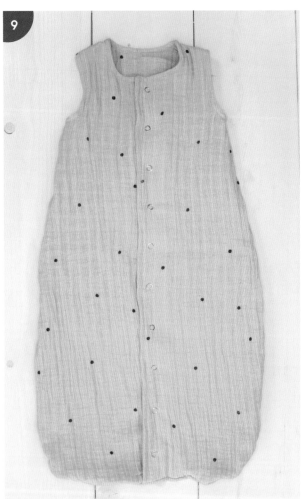

7. Now keep the "shoulder rings" of the front piece as they and insert into the "shoulder rings" of the back piece and secure in place.

8. First pull one shoulder out of the sleeping bag through the opening for turning. You should see the shoulder pieces positioned inside each other. If their right sides are together, then you have done everything right and can now simply sew them together. Proceed in the same manner for the other shoulder.

9. If you want, stitch the seam again and also around the neckline and the armholes. Remember to close the hole for turning. Now all you need to do is add press studs and ta-dah!

# BATHING PONCHO

**LEVEL OF DIFFICULTY:**
⊛ Easy-peasy

*The bathing poncho is perfect for little and large water babies. This poncho is great at the beach, the seaside, the lakes, or indoor and outdoor swimming pools. It cannot be beaten in terms of practicality for it protects against the sun, wraps up your little one after bathing and dries in no time at all, especially when made from muslin. Your little one is perfectly wrapped up on the way to and from the beach so that you don't need to cart towels around.*

**FABRIC:**

Muslin, waffle cotton and terry cloth

Cuddly and soft waffle cotton was used for the example in the instructions.

**YOU NEED:**

Fabric:

⊛ **Sizes 50-68:** 100 cm

   **Sizes 74-104:** 130 cm

⊛ H250 vilene interfacing

⊛ 1 wooden button, alternatively a press stud

**CUTTING:**

Add a seam allowance of 0.75 cm to the hood, the shoulder seams and the neckline.

If you use a different type of hem, you will have to alter the allowance accordingly.

⊛ 4 hood pieces (mirrored x 2) (sheet 4)

⊛ 1 x front piece cut on the fold (sheet 4)

⊛ 1 x back piece cut on the fold (sheet 4)

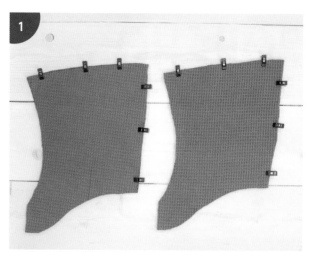

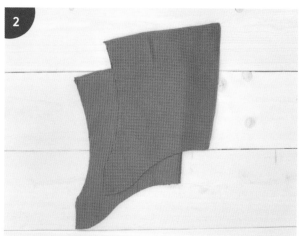

1. First, finish the two hood parts. Sew them together along the clipped edges as shown in the photo. Waffle cotton frays badly so it really needs to be finished therefore I sew it with an overlocker.

2. Next turn one of the hoods inside out and insert the other hood into it so that right sides are together.

3. Now pin and finish the front seam of both hood parts. If you want to attach a button, iron on two small squares of H250 interfacing on the two lower tips.

4. Now turn the hood through the lower edge that is still open. Shape the tips (to do so, you could trim off the corners in the seam allowance) and sew them along the front edge using a straight stitch.

5. Next, take the front and back piece and place them in front of you with right sides together. Sew the shoulder seams on both parts.

6. Now bring the two parts you just created together. Rights sides should be together. Pin the hood onto the neckline of the cloak using the markings on the cut pattern as orientation. When they are on top of each other, the hood should overlap the front neckline. Sew the hood on to the neckline and then finish the seam.

Ensure that you have really sewn through all layers.

7. Your bathing poncho should now look like the photo.

8. Option: as a final step you can make a buttonhole and sew on a button.

**BATHING PONCHO**

# PROJECTS

## AUTUMN
## WINTER

# RIB KNIT BODYSUIT

**LEVEL OF DIFFICULTY:**
⊛ Easy-peasy

*The bodysuit is a garment that belongs in every baby's wardrobe. It is super cute and practical too. Add beautiful and trendy rib knit fabric into the mix, and your passion for sewing baby clothes will be well and truly ignited.*

## FABRIC

Muslin, linen, rib jersey, jersey

For the example shown here, the cuffs are made of rib knit but you can also use cuffing fabric.

## YOU NEED:

**Fabric:**
⊛ **Sizes 50-68:** 50 cm
  **Sizes 74-104:** 70 cm
⊛ Three press studs
⊛ Vario pliers

## CUTTING:

Add a seam allowance of 0.75 cm all the way round.

⊛ 1 x front piece cut on the fold (sheet 3)
⊛ 1 x back piece cut on the fold (sheet 3)
⊛ 1 x front collar piece (sheet 3)
⊛ 1 x back collar piece (sheet 3)
⊛ 2 x sleeves (sheet 3)
⊛ 2 x sleeve cuff pieces (sheet 3)
⊛ 1 x leg cuff cut on the fold (sheet 3)

> **TIP:**
> *Would you like to make a super sweet version for a little girl? Take a strip of left-over material, finish it, gather it with the sewing machine and attach it to the front of the neckline before making up.*

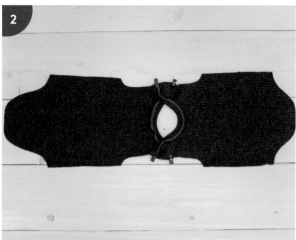

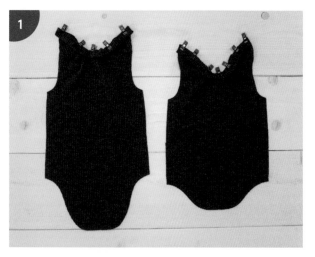

1. Start with the collar pieces for the front and back pieces. The right side of both pieces should be facing up. Fold the collar pieces in half lengthways and stretch to pin them to the neckline. It is best to start at the ends, then mark the centre and distribute the remaining fabric in both directions. Ensure that the shoulder areas are not stretched as much as the neck and back areas.

2. Place the two pattern pieces in front of you with the wrong side facing up. Now you have to correctly position the shoulders. The back piece

lies under the front piece.
Pin them together in this order. Pay close attention to the markings on the pattern. For the next step, it is very helpful if you can use your sewing machine to sew them in place with a few stitches within the seam allowance. Proceed on both sides in this way.

3. Now turn the body so that the right side is facing you. Pin and then sew the two sleeves into the arm holes with right sides together. Follow the markings. (For the small sizes, it is sensible to attach the cuff to the "open" sleeve now, and

then to finish it together with the sleeves and sides in the next step. Otherwise, it becomes very tricky).

4. Now, you can sew the sleeves and sides of the bodysuit in one step.

5. Now, all that is missing are the cuffs on the sleeves and the leg opening. Sew each of the three parts together to form a ring, and fold so the wrong sides are together.

6. Attach the cuffs to the sleeves and the lower opening. For the long strip, be aware that more fabric is required on the back part than at the front. Use pins to secure it.

7. In the final step, mark the position of the press studs and attach three press studs.

8. Now, your beautiful baby bodysuit is finished.

# TROUSERS WITH BUTTON PLACKET

**LEVEL OF DIFFICULTY:**
⊛ Easy-peasy

*One pair of trousers, so many possibilities. Your choice of fabric makes this pair of trousers completely unique and wearable in all seasons. You can make winter trousers from thick, warming cotton fabric or make shorts out of airy muslin for the summer. Sew this casual and easy-to-make design in a variety of fabrics to give your little one their own style.*

## FABRIC:

Muslin, linen, cord, waffle cotton and many more cotton weaves

A soft cotton weave with an elegant pattern was used for the example in the instructions.

## YOU NEED:

**Fabric:**
⊛ **Sizes 50-68:** 45 cm
  **Sizes 74-104:** 65 cm
⊛ 2 cm wide elastic for waistband
⊛ 3 buttons
⊛ Optional: wondertape to secure the button placket

## CUTTING:

Add a seam allowance of 0.75 cm all the way round.
⊛ 1 x waistband cut on the fold (sheet 4)
⊛ 1 x front piece cut on the fold (sheet 4)
⊛ 1 x back piece cut on the fold (sheet 4)
⊛ 1 x button placket (sheet 4)

**Hem allowance**
Add a hem allowance of 2 cm to the legs (long and short design)

| Size | Length of elastic |
|---|---|
| 50/56 | 34 cm |
| 62/68 | 39 cm |
| 74/80 | 42 cm |
| 86/92 | 46 cm |
| 98/104 | 48 cm |

(All measurements are intended as a guide; it is best to measure and try on your child.)

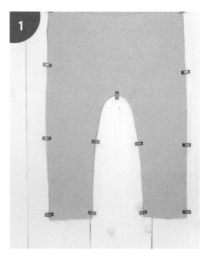

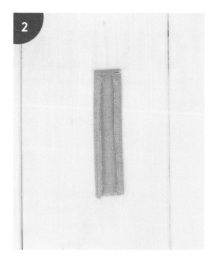

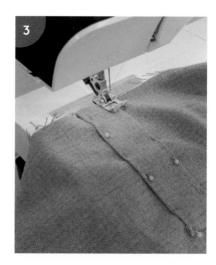

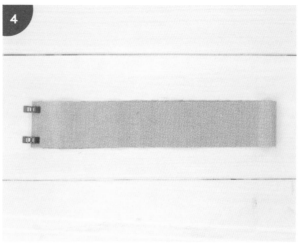

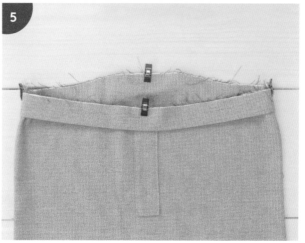

1. Place the front and back pieces over each other with right sides together. Pin the side seams and the crotch seam and sew both pieces together.

2. In the next step, you will prepare the button placket. Finish the edges using zigzag stitch or an overlocker. Now fold back or iron back all visible edges (two long and one short) by approximately 0.5 cm. At this point, wondertape can be a great help. I use it here to stick the button placket to the trousers so that nothing slips.

3. Secure the button placket in the middle of the front part of the trousers. In addition to the wondertape, I also used a couple of pins. The short side, which has not been folded, should be flush with the top edge of the trousers. Ensure that the button placket is straight to give a great finished look. Now sew it in place on the trousers with stitches close to the edge. Wait until the end to sew on the buttons because they will get in the way when finishing the garment.

4. Now we will work on the trousers' waistband. First sew it together along the short edge with right sides together.

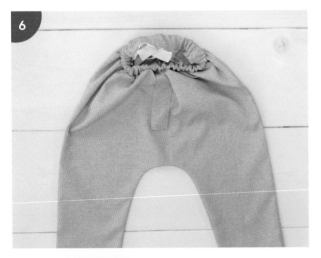

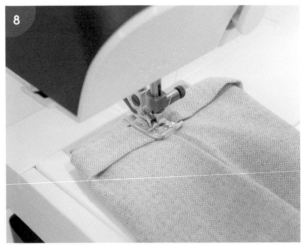

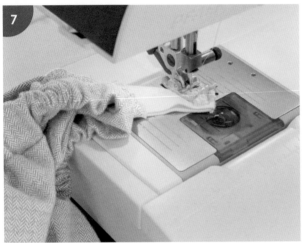

5. You should now have a ring that has the same diameter as the trousers. Fold it in half lengthways (wrong sides facing). The trousers have the right side facing out. Pin and sew the waistband to the top edge of the trousers. In this step, leave an opening of approximately 4 cm.

6. Thread a suitable length of elastic through the opening in the waistband.

7. With a seam allowance of 1 cm on each end, sew the elastic together using a stretch stitch. At this point, pay attention that the elastic is properly positioned in the waistband and has not become twisted.

Then sew the opening in the waistband closed.

8. Finish the legs and decide what type of hem you would like to use. I like to use the turn-up hem. Finally sew all three buttons on the button placket.

9. Now you have completed an absolutely wonderful pair of trousers. Depending on your chosen material, they will be relaxed, summery or elegant.

# BOILED WOOL BAGGY TROUSERS

**LEVEL OF DIFFICULTY:**
◉ Easy-peasy

*These baggy trousers made of boiled wool are perfect for wild games in the fresh air. Quick to take on and off, they offer your little one a lot of freedom. They are casual and comfortable, and keep your child warm, even on cold days.*

**FABRIC:**
Boiled wool
Sweatshirt fabric, jersey, French terry

**YOU NEED:**
Fabric:
● **Sizes 50-68:** 30 cm
  **Sizes 74-104:** 45 cm
● Cuffing fabric
● Optional: a button

**CUTTING:**
Add a seam allowance of 0.75 cm all the way round.

Boiled wool:
● 1 x trouser piece cut on the fold (sheet 2)

Cuffing fabric:
● 1 x waistband cut on the fold (sheet 2)
● 1 x leg cuffs (sheet 2)

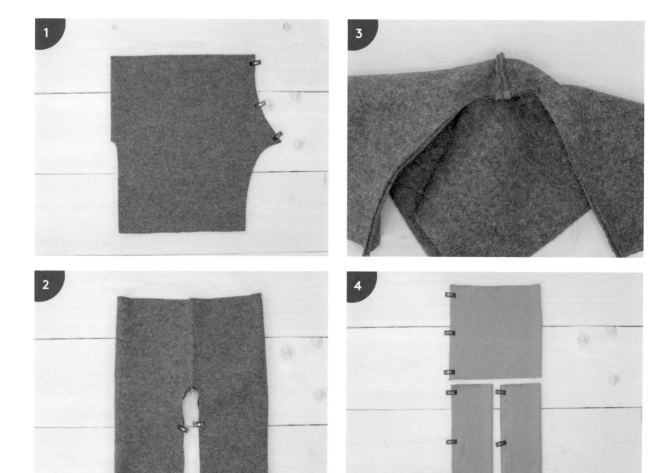

1. Fold the trouser piece cut on the fold in half so that right sides are together and sew the back seam.

2. Unfold the trousers so that the original fold is now at the front in the centre and is positioned over the back seam, allowing two legs to be created. Pin the crotch seam and sew together.

3. When sewing, ensure that you unfold the places where the boiled wool seams meet so that they lie as flat as possible.

4. Now it is time to attach the waistband and cuffs. Sew each of the three pieces of cuffing fabric lengthways with right sides together. Then turn them so that the wrong sides are together, and they are ready for use.

**BOILED WOOL BAGGY TROUSERS**

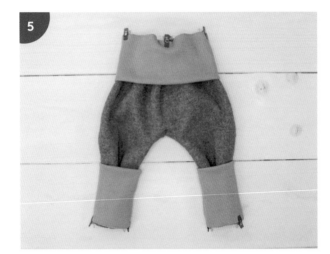

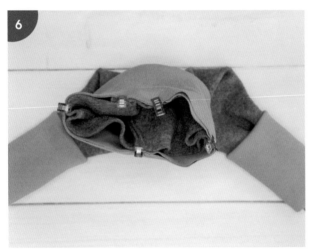

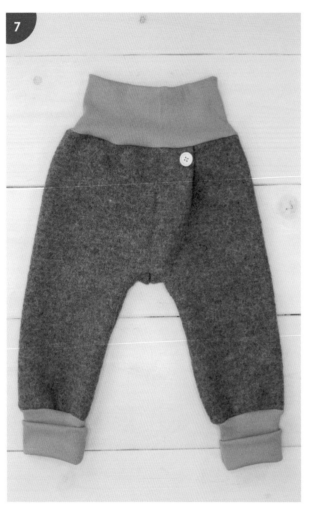

5. Turn the trousers and secure the waistband and cuffs in the right positions (right sides together, with unfinished edges together). Starting from the back seam, the centre of the front and the sides, distribute the cuff fabric evenly around the trousers.

6. If you want to add a button, then make a fold in the material at the front where you can position the button to decorate the trousers once they have been sewn.

7. Sew the waistband and cuffs to the trousers, paying attention that you sew through all the layers. Finally, sew the button into the fold.

# BOILED WOOL WRAP-AROUND JACKET

**LEVEL OF DIFFICULTY:**
⊛ Easy-peasy

*This beautiful wrap-around jacket is made of boiled wool. It is perfect for all seasons: to wear on its own from spring to autumn or as an additional layer in winter. The straps guarantee a good fit and allow it to grow with your child for a long time, so that you will have a lot of pleasure from this piece.*

**FABRIC:**
Boiled wool

**YOU NEED:**
Fabric:
⊛ **Sizes 50-68:** 40 cm
   **Sizes 74-104:** 100 cm
⊛ Some different fabric to be used for the four straps (jersey, French terry, muslin)
⊛ One button

**CUTTING:**
Add a seam allowance of 0.75 cm all the way round.

There is no hem or seam allowance on the sleeve seam and the lower edge because for this project the boiled wool is used without a seam.

Boiled wool:
⊛ 2 x front pieces (mirrored) (sheet 1)
⊛ 1 x back piece cut on the fold (sheet 1)
⊛ 2 x sleeves (mirrored) (sheet 1)
⊛ 2 x squares approximately 2 x 2 cm
Different fabric:
4 straps, length approximately 25-30 cm

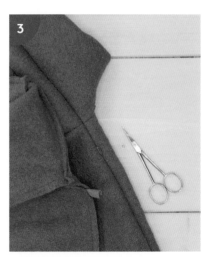

1. Place the back and front pieces on top of each other with right sides together and sew together at the shoulders. The boiled wool can be sewn really well with a normal sewing machine.

2. Next open up the three pieces and use the markings to pin the sleeves in to the armholes with right sides together and sew in place. A self-erasing marker or some chalk can be helpful here.

3. Now pin the sleeves and the sides together. Insert two of the four straps into the seam here. You can find the exact positions on the cut pattern and draw them on with a self-erasing marker. Pay attention that one strap leads inside the jacket and one strap leads outside the jacket.

4. You can simply snip off the protruding part of the strap from the outside.

5. Now fold in the straight edges of both front pieces by 0.5 cm and sew in place close to the edge.

6. Do the same along the curved edge around the neck.

7. Now all that is missing is the two straps on the two front pieces. Place the straps on the wrong side of the front piece, as shown in the image. Then pin a small square of boiled wool over each of them.

8. Use a straight stitch on your sewing machine to sew once around the outer edges of the squares and then secure with a cross in the centres. The straps are now well secured.

9. Finally, you can give the bottom edge and sleeve edges a decorative finish by sewing along the edge using a stretch stitch at one machine foot from the edge. Additionally, you can sew on a button to the top of the front piece where the square is attached on the wrong side. That is an option, but you can also leave off the button.

# RIB KNIT LEGGINGS

**LEVEL OF DIFFICULTY:**
⊛ Easy-peasy

*Leggings are a must for every wardrobe. They are practical with many uses and are an indispensable garment for little ones. Plain or colourful, on their own or under bloomers, there is no limit to your creativity. The waistband is easy to sew, and the leg cuffs mean they grow with your child.*

**FABRIC:**
Rib knit, but also velvety jersey, French terry.

**YOU NEED:**
Fabric:
⊛ **Sizes 50-68:** 40 cm
  **Sizes 74-104:** 60 cm
⊛ Elastic 2 cm wide
⊛ Safety pin

**CUTTING:**
Add a seam allowance of 0.75 cm all the way round.
⊛ 2 x trouser pieces (mirrored) (sheet 4)
⊛ 1 x waistband cut on the fold (sheet 4)
⊛ 2 x leg cuffs (mirrored) (sheet 4)
⊛ Length of elastic for the waistband as follows from the chart below

| Size | Waist |
|------|-------|
| 50/56 | 34 cm |
| 62/68 | 39 cm |
| 74/80 | 42 cm |
| 86/92 | 46 cm |
| 98/104 | 48 cm |

(All measurements are intended as a guide; it is best to measure and try on your child.)

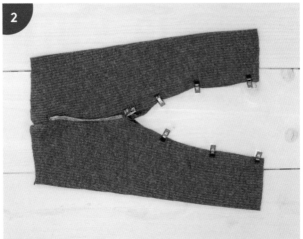

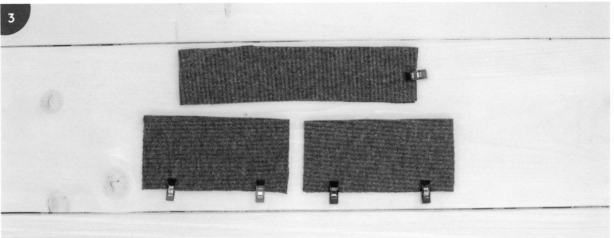

1. Place the two trouser pieces on top of each other with right sides together. Sew the front and back seams.

2. Fold the pieces so that the two seams from step one is on top of each other. You should now be able to see the shape of the legs and therefore the crotch seam. Pin or clip this seam in place, and feel free to use more clips or pins than normal because this seam should later ensure the leggings fit well. The front and back seams should be positioned exactly on top of each other.

3. Now create the waistband and the leg cuffs by sewing them together along the run of the thread with right sides together.

4. Turn the trousers the right way round and sew the folded-over waistband with the raw edges to the trousers with right sides together. Leave an opening of 4 cm for the elastic. Now sew the leg cuffs to the legs with right sides and raw edges together.

5. Using a safety pin, thread the elastic through the waistband and sew the two ends of it together with a seam allowance of 1 cm on each side using a stretch jersey stitch. Pay attention that the elastic is not twisted. Finally sew the opening closed.

6. So that the elastic does not end up twisted later on, I also secure it in the waistband with a few stitches on the left and right.

# BOILED WOOL MINI JACKET

**LEVEL OF DIFFICULTY:**

⊛ ⊛ ⊛ Spend some time and effort for wonderful results!

*This jacket is for all little ones who love nature. This coat equips your tots for fun and wild games in the open air. Thanks to a generous cut, it fits comfortably and the longer back keeps them warm. It is guaranteed to keep them smiling!*

**FABRIC:**

Outer fabric:
Boiled wool

Lining:
Muslin, waffle cotton, jersey, French terry

**YOU NEED:**

Outer fabric and lining:
⊛ **Sizes 50-68:** 70 cm
  **Sizes 74-80:** 80 cm
  **Sizes 86-104:** 100 cm

⊛ H250 vilene interfacing
⊛ Buttons
  **Sizes 50-92:** four buttons
  **Size 98-104:** five buttons

**Optional:**
20 cm cuffing fabric for sizes 98/104

**CUTTING:**

Add a seam allowance of 0.75 cm all the way round.

Outer fabric:
⊛ 1 x back piece cut on the fold (sheet 1)
⊛ 2 x front pieces (mirrored) (sheet 1)
⊛ 2 x sleeves (mirrored) (sheet 1)
⊛ 2 x hood pieces (mirrored) (sheet 1)

Lining:
⊛ 1 x back piece cut on the fold (sheet 1)
⊛ 2 x front pieces (mirrored) (sheet 1)
⊛ 2 x sleeves (mirrored) (sheet 1)
⊛ 2 x hood pieces (mirrored) (sheet 1)

Optional cuffing fabric:
⊛ 2 x pieces for sleeve cuffs (sheet 1)

**TIP:**

*In the pattern sheet, the sleeve is the basic pattern for the option with the cuffs. If you want to make the design with turned up sleeves, then you have to extend the sleeve by the length of the cuff and the desired length of your turn up (pattern piece sleeve plus cuff length plus turn-up length).*

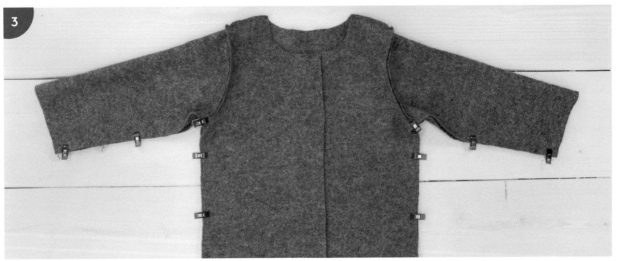

1. Start with the outer jacket. Place the two front parts on top of the back part with right sides together. Sew both shoulder seams.

2. Spread the three pattern pieces out in front of you so that the right sides are facing up. Take a sleeve and pin into the armhole according to the markings on the pattern. Do the same for the other sleeve and sew both sleeves in place.

3. Turn the jacket inside out and sew the outer seams of the arm and sides on both sides. Ensure that where the boiled wool seams meet, they can be folded flat.

4. Sew the two hood pieces together.

5. Pin the hood to the neck of the jacket with right sides together. Observe the markings on the pattern and sew in place.

6. We will now sew the lining. Place the two front parts on top of the back part with right sides together. Sew both shoulder seams.

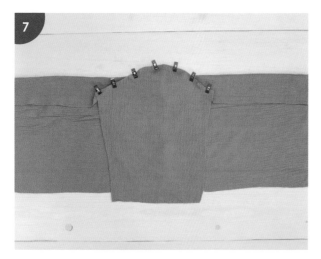

7. Spread the three pattern pieces out in front of you so that the right sides are facing up. Take a sleeve and pin into the armhole according to the markings on the pattern. Do the same for the other sleeve and sew both sleeves in place.

8. Turn the jacket inside out and sew the outer seams of the arm and sides on both sides. In one sleeve leave a turning hole of approximately 10 cm.

9. Sew the two parts of the hood together.

**BOILED WOOL MINI JACKET**

10. Pin the hood to the neck of the jacket with right sides together. Pay attention to the markings on the pattern and sew in place.

11. Now insert all of the outer jacket into the inner jacket with right sides together and pin together on all outer edges. Now you can choose between the overlocker or the sewing machine. For the following example, I used the overlocker to sew my pinned edges (and therefore also the jacket).

12. Now iron on two strips of H250 interfacing on the wrong side of both side edges of the lining. This is for the button placket.

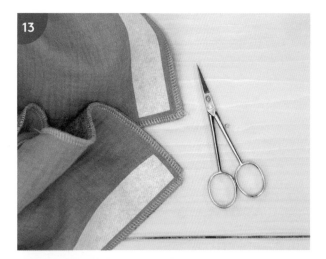

13. Trim the corner tips in the seam. If you have used the overlocking stitch for this part, you will have to undo a few stitches and add a few stitches with the sewing machine before trimming.

14. I always resew the seam area where the front part of the jacket meets the extended back piece. It means that you can push out the curve more easily and everything is securely sewn.

15. Pull the jacket through the opening in the sleeve so that right sides face out. Pin the edges where the lining and the outer jacket meet and sew around the whole jacket at the width of the sewing foot or near to the edge according to taste. For this step work slowly and carefully so that the end result will be even nicer.

16. Carefully insert the arms of the lining into the outer jacket and use pins to hold in place with the seams over each other (wrong sides together) on the lower part of the sleeve. Pull the pins through the turning and pull out the end of the sleeve.

17. Unpin and adjust the layers of fabric so that the right sides are together. Secure this position and then pin the rest of the armhole in the same manner.

Sew the end of the sleeve together. Do the same for the other sleeve. Then sew up the opening for turning.

18. Mark out the buttonholes and work them either with the sewing machine foot or manually (you will find a more detailed description at the start of this book under "Sewing Buttonholes"). Alternatively, you could add press studs.

# FOLD-OVER CUFFS FOR BOILED WOOL JACKET AND BOILED WOOL PLAYSUIT

The fold-over cuffs are a great and unbelievably practical alternative to normal cuffs. They keep your little one's fingers and toes warm. Above all for very young children, it is highly recommendable to add this alternative to their sleeve and leg cuffs. Whether they are in a carrycot or in a pram, everything is protected from wind and weather.

When attaching the fold-over cuffs, ensure that they always fold to the same side. I usually sew them so that the fold is on the back when their hands and feet are out, and the fold-over cuff comes forward to cover hands and feet.

**BOILED WOOL MINI JACKET**

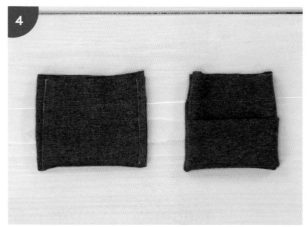

1. Start with the normal cutting pattern for the legs or sleeves and half it in the direction of the run of the thread. Mirror cut the piece plus the seam allowance (piece 1). Now you need the matching pieces which you use to make the fold-over. To do so, extend the cut pattern piece by one half exactly (pattern piece 1 plus 0.5 pattern piece 1) and mirror cut it out (piece 2).

2. Now place both short pieces in front of you with the right side facing up. Fold the long pieces in half with wrong sides together. You should now have one open and one closed side. Place the open side flush against the bottom side of the short cuff piece. Do the same for the second cuff.

3. Now fold the short cuff piece from the bottom up towards the top edge (the long cuff with the closed fold on the inside is positioned in the middle of this fold). Repeat this step for the second cuff. Sew both sides using the stretch stitch on your sewing machine. Ensure that you include all the layers. Trim the seam allowance.

4. In the final step, everything becomes clear. Turn the cuffs the right way out. They should now look like the photo. If you have made it to here, then sewing them to the jacket should be child's play.

# BOILED WOOL PLAYSUIT

**LEVEL OF DIFFICULTY:**

⊗ ⊗ ⊗ Spend some time and effort for wonderful results!

*In this playsuit your tots are perfectly protected from the weather and also super cute to look at. This mini playsuit made from boiled wool is definitely worth the effort. Your little one can wear it the entire autumn and winter season and it will keep them nice and warm in the carrycot, in the pram or on their own two feet.*

**FABRIC:**

**Outer fabric:**
Boiled wool

**Lining:**
Muslin, Jersey, French terry

**YOU NEED:**

**Outer fabric and lining:**
- **Sizes 50-68:** 95 cm
  **Sizes 74-80:** 105 cm
  **Sizes 86-104:** 140 cm
- H250 vilene interfacing
- Buttons
  **Sizes 50-68:** four buttons
  **Sizes 74-92:** five buttons
  **Sizes 98-104:** six buttons
- Cuffing fabric for sizes 98/104: 45 cm
  (more if you add the fold-over cuffs)

**CUTTING:**

Add a seam allowance of 0.75 cm all the way round.

**Outer fabric:**
- 1 x back piece cut on the fold (sheet 3)
- 2 x front pieces (mirrored) (sheet 3)
- 2 x sleeves (mirrored) (sheet 3)
- 2 x hood pieces (mirrored) (sheet 3)

**Lining:**
- 1 x back piece cut on the fold (sheet 3)
- 2 x front pieces (mirrored) (sheet 3)
- 2 x sleeves (mirrored) (sheet 3)
- 2 x hood pieces (mirrored) (sheet 3)

**Cuffing fabric:**
- 1 x hood cuff cut on the fold (sheet 3)
- 2 x sleeve cuffs (mirrored) (sheet 3)
- 2 x leg cuffs (mirrored) (sheet 3)

> **TIP:**
> *The fold-over cuffs (see tutorial) are a great alternative to normal cuffs. They keep the smallest toddlers and babies toasty warm and perfectly protect them from wind and weather.*

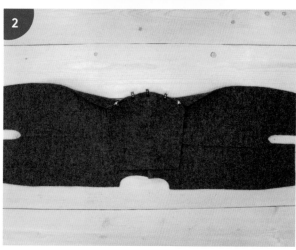

1. Start with the outer piece. Place the two front parts on top of the back part with right sides together. Sew both shoulder seams.

2. Spread the three pattern pieces out in front of you so that the right sides are facing up. Take a sleeve and pin into the armhole according to the markings on the pattern. Do the same for the other sleeve and sew both sleeves in place.

3. Turn the playsuit inside out and sew the outer seams of the arm and sides. Ensure that where the boiled wool seams meet, they can be folded flat.

4. Sew the hood pieces together.

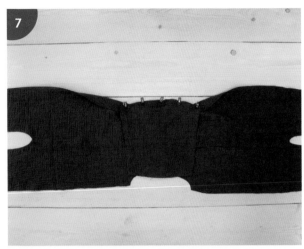

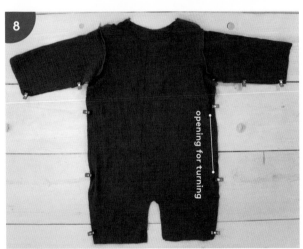

5. Pin the hood to the neck of the playsuit with right sides together. Observe the markings on the pattern and sew in place.

6. Now we will sew the lining. Place the two front parts on top of the back part with right sides together. Sew both shoulder seams.

7. Spread the three pattern pieces out in front of you so that the right sides are facing up. Take a sleeve and pin into the armhole according to the markings on the pattern. Do the same for the other sleeve and sew both sleeves in place.

8. Turn the playsuit inside out and sew the outer seams of the arm and side seams on both sides. In one side leave a turning hole of approximately 12 cm.

9.  Sew the two parts of the hood together.

10. Pin the hood to the neck of the playsuit with right sides together. Pay attention to the markings on the pattern and sew in place.

11. Now insert all of the outer playsuit into the inner playsuit with right sides together. Pay attention around the hood. Fold the hood cuff in half lengthways and pin it with the raw edge between the two hood pieces. Let the ends grow thinner towards the neck seam.

12. To sew the two pieces together, you can choose between the overlocker or the sewing machine. For the following, I used the overlocker to sew from the lower tip of the left front piece to the lower tip of the right front piece. The lower part remains open. Now iron on two strips of H250 interfacing on the wrong side of both side edges of the lining. This is for the button placket.

**BOILED WOOL PLAYSUIT**

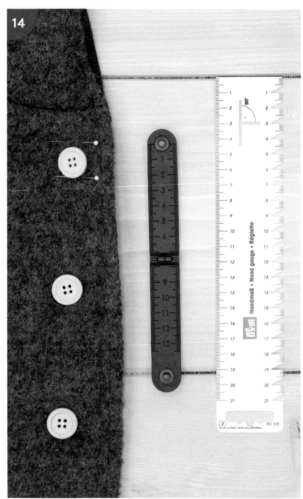

13. Turn the playsuit the right way again. Begin sewing 2 cm from the crotch. Sew around the central opening and then stop approximately 2 cm from the crotch. Sew approximately the width of one sewing machine foot from the edge. The more carefully you work here, the more beautiful the playsuit will be.

14. If you have decided to add buttons and button holes, you should do this now. Use a hand gauge and pins. (You can find more detailed instructions at the start of the book under "Sewing Buttonholes") If you are using press studs, you could also simply attach them at the end.

15. Turn the playsuit again so that the boiled wool side at the bottom. Now we will sew the legs. To do so, pin the leg pieces made of boiled wool together and sew together. Do the same with the muslin leg pieces. Only sew the straight edge of the crotch because the round crotch seam in the middle will only be sewn together at the end.

16. When sewing the crotch seam, the correct placement of the fabric is very important. The two parts of the button placket must be placed over each other and be sewn together with the rest of the suit. It is important that the layers are positioned on top of each other exactly as is shown in the photo: boiled wool playsuit back piece, then the boiled wool button placket with muslin with right side up, then boiled wool button placket with muslin with wrong side up and finally the back piece of the playsuit lining. Pin the layers as described.

17. Sew the seam in three stages: 1. Sew all layers with a straight stitch within the seam allowance. Be extra careful to ensure you have sewn all layers (looking through the turning opening on the right side may help).2. Sew the seam again with a stretch stitch and pay attention that you sew right up to the leg seam so that everything is securely sewn there. 3. Finally, finish the opening with a zig-zag stitch.

18. Now sew all four cuffs for the sleeves and feet. If you want to use fold-over cuffs instead of normal cuffs, you can find a tutorial on page 122 entitled "Fold-over Cuffs for Boiled Wool Jacket And Boiled Wool Playsuit".

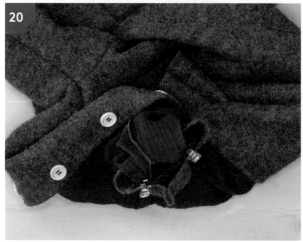

19. Turn the playsuit so the right side is facing out and in the next step, attach all four cuffs.

20. Now attach the cuffs between the layers of the playsuit. (You can find exact instructions at the start of the book under the heading "Neatly Attaching Cuffs Between Layers"). To do so, you will have to pull the sleeves and legs through the turning opening. For all four cuffs, the layers have to be pinned and sewn as shown in the photo in the following order: boiled wool, the cuff with right sides together, then the lining again with right sides together.

21. Now sew up the opening and get outside into the fresh air – you have earned it!

# BOILED WOOL MINI HAT

**LEVEL OF DIFFICULTY:**

◉ Easy-peasy

*This mini hat is a cosy accessory for cold days. Thanks to the straps it will not slip off and it keeps ears warm and protected from the cold wind. It is an easy-to-sew pattern with a really cute point at the end.*

**FABRIC:**

Outer fabric:
Boiled wool

Lining fabric:
Jersey (muslin is also suitable)

**YOU NEED:**

Outer fabric and lining:
◉ **Head circumference 36-44 cm:** 25 cm
  **Head circumference 44-52 cm:** 30 cm
◉ Jersey straps, approximately 25 to 30 cm in length

**CUTTING:**

Add a seam allowance of 0.75 cm all the way round.

Outer fabric:
2 x hat pieces (mirrored) (sheet 2)

Inner fabric:
◉ 2 x hat pieces (mirrored) (sheet 2)
◉ 2 x strips, approximately 3 cm wide and approximately 25-30 cm long

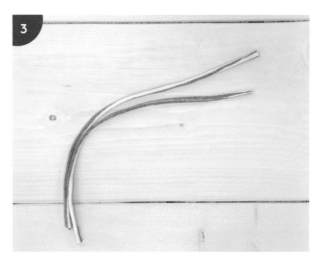

1. Use the sewing machine to sew the pieces of the outer fabric together along the markings.

2. Sew the pieces of the lining together in the same manner. An overlocker will also give good results here. For the inner hat leave a turning opening of approximately 4 cm in the seam at the back.

3. Make the two straps by cutting two approximately 3 cm wide strips from the jersey lining fabric.

4. Now insert the lining hat inside the boiled wool hat with right sides together. In this step also position the straps according to the markings.

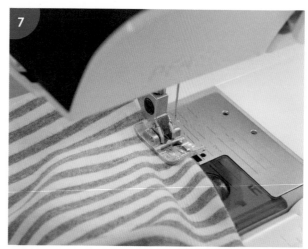

5. Sew the two parts together according to the markings.

6. Turn the hat through the turning opening so that the right side faces out and sew along the already sewn edge.

7. Now sew up the turning opening.

8. The mini hat is now finished!

BOILED WOOL MINI HAT

# BEANIE

**LEVEL OF DIFFICULTY:**

◉ Easy-peasy

*This beanie is a little more relaxed than the Mini Hat. Made out of trendy rib knit fabric, it turns little girls and boys into true trendsetters. It is the prefect accessory for a cosy warm winter outfit.*

**FABRIC:**

Rib knit or ribbed jersey

**YOU NEED:**

Fabric:

◉ **Head circumference 42-50:** 55 cm

  **Head circumference 50-58:** 63 cm

**CUTTING:**

Add a seam allowance of 0.75 cm all the way round.

◉ 1 x hat piece cut on the fold (sheet 3)

**TIP:**

*The pattern for the beanie is also suitable for larger heads. If you like the trendy Mom and Me style, then make yourself a hat to matches your tot.*

*You will both look really cute.*

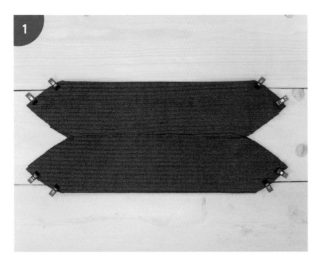

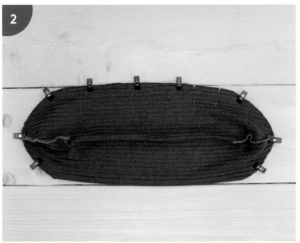

1.  Place the hat piece in front of you with the right side facing up. Fold in half so that tip 1 and tip 2 as well as tip 3 and tip 4 lie flush over each other. Finish all four short sides, which are secured with clips in the photo. The overlocker works well on rib knit. It is better to use a sewing machine for beanies made with thin jersey fabric as otherwise the seams may be visible, which does not look as nice.

2.  Place the hat so that on each side the two seams are over each other. Now sew the curve by pinning and sewing the still open seam starting at the front middle via the seam at the back and towards the front middle of the doubled inner piece. Leave a turning opening of 4 cm.

3.  Ensure that the meeting seams are really neatly laid over each other and position the seams mirror-inverted to each other so that they lie as flat as possible.

4. Before turning, sew the overlock seam and in the same step, sew the curve. The more curved the seams are, the better the hat will fit on the head.

5. Turn the beanie the right way round and sew up the turning opening close to the edge.

6. Push the two halves of the beanie into each other. The sewn-up turning opening is on the inside.

# ACKNOWLEDGEMENTS

*If one year ago, someone had told me that I would be working on this project, I would have laughed out loud. I received an email from EMF publishing house and many things changed. As a result, this passion project has come to life.*

### Marc

Thank you from the bottom of my heart. You are the absolute best; without you I would not have had the courage to see this project through. We are a super team, something that the past few months have again confirmed.

### Jette, Ida & Bruno

You are the basis for all of these patterns, my inspiration and my greatest treasures.

### Mama & Papa

Thank you for the roots, thank you for the wings and thank you for the weekends where you kept our backs free. And thank you Mama for the unforgettable trip to Munich City.

### Kira

Thank you for sending that email. Thank you for your confidence in us and for the many fun telephone calls. Even though I was often a nervous wreck, I could still always laugh with you and be refreshed to tackle the next step. Thank you for the wonderful day in Marsraum.

### Meritt

You understood what we are about and have shown it perfectly in the graphics and design – minimal, authentic and beautiful.

### Solveigh

You are the basis for the core of this book. These nineteen wonderful patterns have occasionally shattered our nerves. Thank you for your calm, your peace and your humour, which have carried our collaboration.

### Denise, Marina, Kathrin

Thank you for your time, your experience and your sewing machine skills.

### Patrick & Minimodels

What a wonderful day in December 2019, just before Christmas in the Marsraum meeting space in Munich. The most delicious coffee with the nicest people. And boys, girls and your moms, you rocked the place!

### You

Thank you for buying this book.

Thank you to the many kind people who are loyal to us on Instagram and show a real interest in our work. Every like, every comment and every order give us strength and provides new inspiration. THANK YOU to every individual, without you this book would not exist.

### Sponsor

Lotta&Emil – Thank you from the bottom of our hearts for your support. Your shoes give feel good vibes in spring, summer, autumn and winter (lottaundemil.de).

It's a mom thing – Jule, you lovely thoroughbred mother and mompreneur with the most beautiful baby accessories (itsamomthing.de).

Echt-anziehend for fabric from which dreams are made... How lovely that we got to know each other (echtanziehend.de).

Nähzentrum Eilers – for the best customer service and the best Pfaff sewing machines, which simply do what they should (nähzentrum-eilers.de).

Prym Deutschland – for the high-quality sewing accessories, which means the best hobby in the world gives twice as much enjoyment (prym.com).

# ABOUT THE AUTHOR

Since the author could think, her head has been full of new ideas, thoughts and creative energy. Fabric, colours, creative activity and now also a lively family life: that is her world and that is what she loves.

After her studies, career and the birth of her three children, her passion for sewing came increasingly to the fore. At first, she designed clothes for her children. People around her soon became interested in the finished clothes and so together with her husband, she established the children's fashion label JULESNaht.

Her brand stands for practical and comfortable children's fashion that is simple and beautiful with a special something. It is clothing that is made for free and wild games.

Elegant and made with a lot of love – that is her motto. And that is how she and her husband live: with creative hands on the sewing machine and a creative head in the background. Today, they run a small but beautiful online shop and their handmade clothes make young and old happy.

**Julika and Marc, the people behind JULESNaht**

**Tuva Publishing**
www.tuvapublishing.com

**Address** Merkez Mah. Cavusbasi Cad. No:71
Cekmekoy - Istanbul 34782 / Turkey
Tel: +9 0216 642 62 62

**Mini Fashion**

**First Print** 2022 / June

All Global Copyrights Belong To
Tuva Tekstil ve Yayıncılık Ltd.

**Content** Sewing

**Editor in Chief** Ayhan DEMİRPEHLİVAN
**Project Editor** Kader DEMİRPEHLİVAN
**Designer** Julika LANDERMANN
**Technical Editor** Leyla ARAS
**Graphic Designers** Ömer ALP, Abdullah BAYRAKÇI,
Tarık TOKGÖZ
**Photograph** Tuva Publishing

**ISBN** 978-605-7834-63-8

Edition Michael Fischer GmbH, 2021
www.emf-verlag.de

This translation of HEJ. MINIMODE - KLEIDUNG NAHEN FÜR BABYS UND
KLEINKKINDER first published in GERMANY by Edition Michael Fischer
GmbH in 2021 is published by arrangement with Silke Bruenink Agency,
Munich Germany.

 TuvaYayincilik  TuvaPublishing

 TuvaYayincilik  TuvaPublishing